THE
PRESIDENTS
OF THE
UNITED STATES

THE
PRESIDENTS
OF THE
UNITED STATES

Samuel Crompton

SMITHMARK

This edition published in 1995
by SMITHMARK Publishers Inc.,
16 East 32nd Street
New York, New York 10016

SMITHMARK books are available for bulk purchase
for sales promotion and premium use. For details
write or telephone the Manager of Special Sales,
SMITHMARK Publishers Inc., 16 East 32nd Street,
New York, NY 10016. (212) 532-6600.

Produced by Brompton Books Corp.,
15 Sherwood Place
Greenwich, CT 06830

ISBN 0-8317-7074-0

Printed in China

10 9 8 7 6 5 4 3

Picture Credits
All pictures are courtesy of the Bettmann Archive, except for
the following:
Adams National Historic Site: 10-11; Brompton Picture
Library: 11 right, 13 bottom, 25 top left, 27 bottom right, 30
top right, 50 bottom, 56 right, 57 top, 64 left, 65 bottom, 68
right, 75 bottom right, 76 left; Anne S.K. Brown Military
Collection, Brown University: 21 bottom, 29 top left; Jimmy
Carter Library: 75 both; Dwight D. Eisenhower Library: 66,
67; Bill Fitz-Patrick/The White House: 77 top; Gerald R.
Ford Library: 74 top and bottom right; Rutherford B. Hayes
Presidential Center: 39 bottom right; Thomas Jefferson
Memorial Foundation, Inc./James Tkatch: 13 top; Lyndon B.
Johnson Library: 70 both, 71 both; John F. Kennedy Library:
68 left, 69 both; Library of Congress: 4, 9 bottom, 14, 17
both, 22, 24 bottom right, 28, 34, 35, 36, 37 right, 38 top
right, 40 to and bottom right, 43 left, 45 right, 46-47 top, 47,
48 left, 50 top, 53 top and bottom right, 58 top, 74 left;
National Archives: 33 left, 38 left, 51 bottom, 55 bottom
right; National Portrait Gallery, Smithsonian Institution: 23;
New England Stock Photo, Tony La Gruth ©: 2; New York
Public Library: 30 bottom right; The New-York Historical
Society, New York City: 15 top, 26 bottom right; Nixon
Presidential Materials Project, The National Archives: 72-73,
73 top right; Reuters/Bettmann: 79; Franklin D. Roosevelt
Library and Museum: 56 left; Karl Schumacher/The White
House: 77 bottom; Tennessee State Library and Archives: 21
top; Harry S. Truman Library: 62; Thomas Jefferson Papers,
University of Virginia: 15 bottom; UPI/Bettmann
Newsphotos: 49 right, 51 top, 54 bottom right, 63 top, 72 left,
78 right; U.S. Army Photos: 56 bottom (#MM-Wall-43-
5251), 64 right (163-42-116), 65 top (ETO-HQ-44-4701); U.S.
Military Academy Archives: 38 right; David Valdez/The
White House: 78 left; Valley Forge Historical Society: 8;
Louis A. Warren Lincoln Library and Museum: 33 right;
Wisconsin Center for Film and Theater Research: 76 right

Acknowledgments
The publisher would like to thank the following people who
helped in the preparation of this book: Don Longabucco,
who designed it; Elizabeth Montgomery, who did the picture
research; Florence Norton, who prepared the index; and
John Kirk, who edited the text.

*Page 1: The Capitol, as it
appeared in the 1920s.*

Page 2: The White House.

*Page 4: The inauguration
of Abraham Lincoln.*

CONTENTS

George Washington

(1732-99)

First President
of the United States

Term of Office: April 30, 1789-March 3, 1797
First Lady: Martha Dandridge Custis
Vice President: John Adams

Washington was born on February 22, 1732, at Pope's Creek in Westmoreland County, Virginia. The Washington family has been traced as far back as 1260 in England, when the family name was de Wessington; Washington's great-grandfather had come to Virginia from England in 1656 or 1657, thus establishing the family's American branch. Washington's father, Augustine Washington, died when George was 11 years old, leaving George and his two sisters, three brothers, and several half-brothers and sisters.

George Washington's formal schooling lasted only until he was about 15, after which he became an assistant to local surveyors. George's half-

To his countrymen and to most historians George Washington seems almost to have been created for the great tasks entrusted to him. In 1789 he was given the executive leadership of a new nation that was embarking on an unprecedented democratic experiment. In his time as chief executive Washington both set many precedents and endowed the presidency with dignity and respect. Although he doubtless made some errors and was not universally loved, he nevertheless guided the new United States through one of the most critical eight-year periods in its history. Washington often confessed that he felt unequal to his responsibilities, but by virtue of his intelligence, magnanimous spirit, and great character this great American established himself as "first in war, first in peace, and first in the hearts of his countrymen."

brother, Lawrence Washington, was the principal heir of Augustine Washington and had inherited much of the family property. It was Lawrence who named the family homestead Mount Vernon, in memory of his service in Central America under a British admiral named Vernon. When Lawrence died in 1752, George came into possession both of Mount Vernon and a large amount of land.

The young Virginian became known to a larger world through his soldiering in the French and Indian War. In 1753 Virginia Governor Robert Dinwiddie sent Washington, by now a militia major, to warn French troops to stay out of western Pennsylvania and Virginia. After being re-buffed by the French commander near Erie, Pennsylvania, Washington urged Dinwiddie to build a fort at the junction of the Allegheny and Ohio rivers, present-day Pittsburgh. Before Washington arrived at the site of the new fort, French forces captured it and renamed it Fort Duquesne. Washington pressed on toward the site, and on May 28, 1754, his militia unit fought a skirmish with French troops. Ten Frenchmen were killed, including the French commander.

Washington and his men then built a defensive work called Fort Necessity, but a larger French force besieged it, and Washington surrendered under honorable terms on July 4, 1754, whereupon

Below: At harvest time Washington supervises work at his plantation home, Mount Vernon.

Above: At Valley Forge, Washington reviews his ragged army during the grim winter of 1777-78.

he and his men returned to Virginia. His first command had thus been something of a failure. Although in the following year he was present at the defeat of Braddock's army by the French near Fort Duquesne, Washington ultimately had the satisfaction of being a leader of the force that at last captured the troublesome fort in 1758, thus ending the threat to Pennsylvania and Virginia.

After the French and Indian War, Washington married Martha Dandridge Custis and increased the size of his landholdings by adding Martha's to his own. As a member of the Virginia House of Burgesses, Washington spoke and wrote of the need for the American colonies to obtain more rights than they then had under British rule. When at last the colonies rebelled the Second Continental Congress in 1775 quickly chose Washington as general and commander-in-chief of the rapidly-forming American armies.

The new American leader faced enormous problems during his period as commander-in-chief. Although he suffered a number of defeats from more experienced British commanders, he managed to keep his army intact, even through two deadly winters. Finally, in 1781, Washington's Continentals and French army units combined with a French fleet to trap and completely surround British General Charles Cornwallis's 7000-man army at Yorktown, Virginia. When Cornwallis surrendered the war was effectively over, although the peace treaty was not signed until 1783. Washington emerged from the war with an immense national and international reputation, everywhere hailed as the modern Cincinnatus, the patriotic farmer-turned-soldier who had saved his nation but was above sordid personal ambition.

In 1787 Washington also presided over the convention that wrote the United States Constitution. Following this work, he was elected president in the first United States presidential election. At the age of 57 Washington was inaugurated on April 30, 1789, at Federal Hall in New York city.

Washington believed in the separation of powers: a Chief Executive, the Congress, and the Supreme Court. He created the first presidential cabinet and the departments of foreign affairs, war and treasury. He was deeply distressed by the animosity that developed between Alexander Hamilton, the head of the Treasury, and Thomas Jefferson, the minister of foreign affairs, and he could not prevent their rivalry from creating the nation's first defined political parties – the Federalists and the Democratic-Republicans.

The rise of partisan politics was by no means the only problem that beset Washington's administration. There was also a threat from the pirate states in North Africa, which sometimes captured American ships and held Americans for ransom. Although it offended his personal and patriotic pride, Washington agreed to a treaty that paid $800,000 in ransom and promised $24,000 in yearly tribute to the Barbary pirates. He also faced turbulence at home; whiskey-makers in western Pennsylvania revolted against the federal government in protest against taxes. Washington organized 15,000 soldiers, and by November 1794 the Whiskey Rebellion had been suppressed.

Tired of the many challenges that confronted him as president, Washington declined to run for a third term. Before going into retirement, he published a Farewell Address to the American people, urging Americans to avoid political party conflict and regional factionalism and to stay clear of entangling alliances with European countries. Washington divided his remaining years between farming and occasional bouts of public service. He had become a legend in his own time, and his advice was sought on numerous occasions. In December, 1799, Washington caught a cold which developed into a serious infection: he died on December 14, 1799. Of his 67 years, perhaps 40 had been spent in public service. His courage was tremendous, his faith firm, and he left a legacy of pride for all Americans.

Left: The inauguration of Washington as first president of the United States, April 30, 1789.

Left: An old comrade-in-arms, the Marquis de Lafayette, pays a call on his former commander at Mount Vernon.

John Adams

(1735-1826)

Second President
of the United States

Term of Office: March 4, 1797-March 3, 1801
First Lady: Abigail Smith
Vice President: Thomas Jefferson

John Adams was the longest-lived American president, surviving long enough to see his son, John Quincy Adams, become the sixth president of the United States. Adams had a volatile, demanding temperament, but he was also known as a sensitive correspondent and an excellent friend and family man.

Adams was born on October 30, 1735, in Braintree, Massachusetts; his great-great grandfather had settled in Boston as far back as the 1630s. Adams was graduated from Harvard in 1755, taught school for a short time, and then studied law. In 1764 he married Abigail Smith. The couple had five children, and John Adams kept up an intimate and engaging correspondence with his wife during the substantial periods of time when they were apart.

In 1770 the fiercely patriotic Adams surprised fellow Bostonians by defending British Army Captain Thomas Preston and his men when they were charged with manslaughter in the Boston Massacre: Adams maintained that the soldiers were only obeying orders. In 1775 Adams helped to bring about the appointment of George Washington as American commander-in-chief. He helped Jefferson edit the Declaration of Independence the following year, and at the end of the Revolutionary War it was he, along with Ben Franklin and John Jay, who negotiated the 1783 Treaty of Paris whereby Great Britain formally recognized American independence.

After serving as George Washington's vice president from 1789-1796, Adams was elected president in his own right in 1796. He was a moderate Federalist; though he believed in a strong national government, he tried to maintain a nonpartisan stance while in office. Adams kept most of the members of Washington's cabinet, which may have been a mistake, since several of them were extreme Federalists and anything but nonpartisan.

In foreign affairs Adams faced and confronted a warlike post-Revolutionary France that had begun to seize American merchant ships that traded with Great Britain. Adams stimulated the construction of new American warships and thereby created the first substantial American navy. The American ships soon gave a good account of themselves,

defeating equal-sized French ships on numerous occasions.

As the undeclared naval war dragged on, Adams presented the Alien and Sedition Acts to Congress, legislation which would allow the president to banish or imprison foreigners living in the United States. Although these laws were not enforced to any great extent, they were considered un-American by many people, and Adams's popularity suffered accordingly. The naval war continued, and Adams named George Washington once again to be commander-in-chief of the American armies. But when it became apparent that Alexander Hamilton, a strong Federalist, would probably gain actual control over the armed forces, Adams backtracked and sent diplomats to France. The envoys came to agreement with the French and signed a treaty on September 30, 1800, thus averting a possible fullscale war.

Adams' popularity was now fairly low, and he lost the election of 1800 to his vice president, Thomas Jefferson. Adams was bitter towards Jefferson, and left Washington on the morning of March 4, 1801, to avoid taking part in the new president's inauguration. Adams retired to Braintree, Massachusetts, and studied history, philosophy, and religion. He and Jefferson later became reconciled and corresponded until shortly before the day they both died, July 4, 1826, fiftieth anniversary of the Declaration of Independence.

Left: Abigail Smith Adams. The perceptive, witty letters written by this delightful first lady are an invaluable source of contemporary U.S. social history.

Left: The birthplaces of two U.S. presidents. That of John Adams is on the right; that of his son, John Quincy Adams, is on the left.

11

Thomas Jefferson

(1743-1826)

Third President of the United States

Term of Office: March 4, 1801-March 3, 1809
First Lady: None (his wife, Martha Skelton, died in 1782)
Vice Presidents: Aaron Burr, George Clinton

Thomas Jefferson, the third president of the United States, actually preferred to be known for other accomplishments. Indeed, there was some logic to that, since the versatile and brilliant Jefferson was also a lawyer, legislator, architect, philosopher, diplomat, and, perhaps above all else, a gifted writer. His second term in office was marred by conflict with Great Britain and possible treason by his former vice president, perhaps one reason why Jefferson preferred to emphasize other aspects of his career.

Jefferson was born on April 13, 1743, in what is now Albermarle County, Virginia. He was the third child in a family of six girls and two boys. When his father died in 1757 Thomas Jefferson, as the oldest male, inherited 2500 acres of land and at least 20 slaves. (It is interesting to note that he later introduced a bill to the Virginia legislature which outlawed the strict use of primogeniture.) Jefferson attended the College of William and Mary and then studied law with George Wythe. As a member of the Virginia House of Burgesses he met George Washington and heard Patrick Henry's rousing speech against the Stamp Act in 1765.

Jefferson designed his own home, the beautiful and famous Monticello, in 1770, and in 1772 he married Martha Wayles Skelton, a widow. The couple had two daughters, Martha died in 1782, and Jefferson never remarried, one of his daughters occasionally acting as hostess in the White House for her father. With the advent of the American Revolution, Jefferson became more political and more noticeable. In 1776 he undertook his single most memorable work – the penning of the Declaration of Independence. As a member of the Second Continental Congress, and a member of a special committee, Jefferson wrote the remarkable document which asserted that men should be free, that governments exist to serve the people, and that when governments fail to do so, the people have the right to revolt. Most of the ideas came from the British tradition of constitutional government, but Jefferson articulated them with unprecedented eloquence.

Left: If Jefferson had done nothing more than design Monticello, his fame would be secure in American history.

Below: The red-haired Jefferson stands with other founding fathers in John Trumbull's well-known work The Signing of the Declaration of Independence.

Jefferson resigned from Congress in that same year and returned to Virginia, where he served as the state governor from 1779 to 1781. (In 1781 he barely escaped capture by British cavalrymen a few months before the battle of Yorktown ended the Revolutionary War.) In 1784 he became the chief American diplomatic representative to France, a post he held long enough to witness the first stirrings of the French Revolution.

In 1789 Jefferson returned to the United States and accepted George Washington's offer to become minister for foreign affairs in the new government. Jefferson feuded with Alexander Hamilton regarding American policy toward Revolutionary France, Jefferson supporting the French revolutionaries, while Hamilton distrusted them and supported Great Britain's war with France. The conflict led Jefferson to resign in 1794.

Between 1796 and 1800 Jefferson served as John Adams' vice president, before becoming president himself in 1801. He served two terms; the first

brought him several important triumphs, while the second brought complications and the loss of some of his popularity. Jefferson stopped the payment of tribute to the Barbary pirates of Tripoli and fought a short, successful naval war against them. In 1803 his representatives in Paris made an extraordinary purchase: for $15 million the United States acquired the Louisiana Territory, thereby doubling the country's size. Jefferson then dispatched Lewis and Clark on their memorable journey across the North American continent, the expedition mapping large areas of the Louisiana Territory and amassing quantities of other valuable information.

In Jefferson's second term Aaron Burr was replaced as vice president by George Clinton, but soon thereafter Burr came under suspicion of trying to seize a large area in the Spanish Southwest for his personal rule. Jefferson acted to have Burr apprehended, imprisoned, and tried for treason, but a strict interpretation of the laws relating to treason allowed Burr to go free.

The second term was beset by other difficulties. Jefferson was caught in the middle of the war between Great Britain and Napoleonic France, and one result was that British ships began impressing American sailors who could not prove their nationality. In 1807 a British ship even fired on an American warship, killing and wounding a number of Americans. Jefferson avoided war and reduced the liklihood of future incidents by declaring an embargo act that prohibited American ships from sailing to foreign ports, but since this measure hurt American shipping, Jefferson lost popularity, especially in New England, which relied on trade. Jefferson was doubtless relieved to end his presidency and retire to Monticello.

Although he was 65, Jefferson led an active retirement, carrying on a large correspondence and entertaining at Monticello. In 1825 the University of Virginia opened its doors, largely as the result of Jefferson's efforts. Jefferson died at Monticello on July 4, 1826. In a self-written epitaph he had said that he hoped he would be remembered as the author of the Declaration of Independence and the Statute of Virginia for religious freedom and as the father of the University of Virginia. He made no reference to the presidency.

Above: Aaron Burr was Jefferson's first vice president. He came so close to winning the 1800 presidential election that the matter had to be decided in the House of Representatives. The House chose Jefferson on the 36th ballot.

Left: Jefferson's front elevation of the rotunda of the University of Virginia.

James Madison

(1751-1836)

Fourth President
of the United States

Term of Office: March 4, 1809-March 3, 1817
First Lady: Dorothea Payne Todd
Vice Presidents: George Clinton, Elbridge Gerry

James Madison was a writer, legislator, and scholar. His presidency was less successful than his work as a legislator and law-maker, for he presided during the difficult period of the War of 1812, when regionalism threatened to pull the Union apart. Madison continued the rule of the "Virginia Dynasty" that included Washington, Jefferson, and Monroe, men who had come of age during the American Revolution and who would guide the new nation up until 1828.

Madison was born in Orange County, Virginia, the eldest of 12 children, on March 16, 1751. He attended the College of New Jersey (later Princeton), where he studied overzealously and suffered from a mild illness between 1771 and 1773. During the Revolution he was named as colonel of the Orange County militia but never served in combat. In 1776, as a delegate to the Virginia legislature, he

Right: Rembrant Peale's famous portrait of the vivacious Dolly Madison.

began his life-long friendship with Thomas Jefferson. He subsequently went to Philadelphia as a member of the Continental Congress and rose to a position of leadership there. In 1783 he initiated the creation of the Library of Congress, which two centuries later would hold the largest collection of books in the world.

Madison also served in the Constitutional Convention of 1787, and his thinking and writing were highly influential in the creation of the United States Constitution. Like Thomas Jefferson, Madison wanted the United States to remain a rural, agricultural country where democracy could continue in its purest form. Madison also served as Jefferson's secretary of state and as a special envoy to France before being elected president in his own right in 1808.

Madison's wife was Dolly Payne Todd, whom he had married in 1794. Dolly was a lively First Lady who delighted in giving large parties and in participating in the social life of the nation's capital. It was a marked shift from the previous administration, during which Jefferson had often dined at the White House alone.

Madison faced his greatest difficulty in relations with Great Britain. The British had long maintained a custom of "impressing" American sailors who could not prove their citizenship for service in the Royal Navy. Madison at first tried to negotiate with the British, but they responded to his overtures too slowly to overtake the war fever that was building in the United States, and in 1812 Madison submitted a request to Congress for a declaration of war on Great Britain.

The War of 1812 proved to be a see-saw contest, with both sides winning small victories but not fully taking advantage of them. Madison soon became unpopular in the New England states, which were hard-hit by the loss of trade. Madison's lowest point came in 1814, when British troops captured and burned Washington itself, but the British left shortly thereafter, and in the next six months

Left: The gutted shell of the White House in 1814, after marauding British troops had put it to the torch.

Below: The bombardment of Fort McHenry by the British on September 13-14, 1814, the incident that inspired Francis Scott Key to compose a song that would become the American national anthem.

Americans won important battles at Baltimore and New Orleans. The war ended as a stalemate, the major issues of impressment and borders still not satisfactorily resolved, but the United States had at least demonstrated its readiness to fight.

Madison left office in 1817 and returned to Virginia. In his long retirement he ran the family plantation and also presided over the University of Virginia. He and his wife had no children. He died on June 28, 1836.

James Monroe

(1758-1831)

Fifth President
of the United States

Term of Office: March 4, 1817-March 7, 1825
First Lady: Elizabeth Kortright
Vice President: Daniel D. Tompkins

Right: A cartoon from the early twentieth-century shows European potentates watching as the U.S. Navy enforces the Monroe Doctrine.

James Monroe was the last of the dynasty of presidents who came from the state of Virginia. He had a remarkable political and diplomatic career which spanned more than 40 years. Foremost among his accomplishments were his participation in the Louisiana Purchase of 1803 and his formulation and expression of the idea that European powers must stay out of both North and South America – later to be called the Monroe Doctrine.

Monroe was born on April 28, 1758 in Westmoreland County, Virginia. He was the oldest of the four boys and one girl in his family. He attended the College of William and Mary but left his studies in order to fight in the Revolutionary War. Fighting in a number of major battles, he distinguished himself with bravery and was wounded in the shoulder at Trenton in 1776.

Following the war Monroe served in the Virginia Assembly and as a member of the Congress of the Confederation between 1783 and 1786. In 1786 he married Elizabeth Kortright, daughter of a New York City merchant. The couple had two daughters and a son who died in infancy.

Monroe's political career accelerated during the early years of the Republic. He served as a United States senator and then as minister to France, appointed by President Washington. Monroe so sympathized with the French revolutionaries as to make partisan statements which brought about his recall in 1796. In 1799 he was elected governor of Virginia, and in 1803 his old friend President Jefferson sent Monroe as an envoy extraordinary to France in order to try to purchase the city of New Orleans. Instead, Monroe and his fellow ambassador, Robert Livingston, managed to purchase the whole Louisiana Territory for only $15 million.

Later he served as minister to Great Britain, and again as governor of Virginia. During the War of 1812 he was secretary of state, and after the burning of Washington, D.C., in 1814 he became the secretary of war as well. Having served in so many capacities, Monroe's election to the presidency in 1816 came as no surprise.

James Monroe was president during the "era of good feelings," a time when there were no severe external threats to the country and when party politics were less acrimonious than before and later. But Monroe did have to grapple with the problem of fighting the Seminole Indians in Florida, appointing General Andrew Jackson to fight, and eventually defeat, the Indians. Spain subsequently sold Florida to the United States for the equivalent of only $5 million dollars. In all, the United States grew from 15 states to 24 states during Monroe's time in office.

Monroe's most famous legacy was the Monroe Doctrine. In December, 1823, in his annual message to Congress, Monroe announced that the United States would resist any attempt of European nations to create new colonies in either North or South America. Although British naval power was essential to backing up the promise, it was Monroe who made the stand and created a definite line between European and American governmental systems.

Monroe had won re-election without opposition in 1820, but he retired at the end of his second term. He lived in Virginia until his wife died in 1830, whereupon he moved to New York City to live with his daughter. He died on July 4, 1831, leaving behind an impressive record.

John Quincy Adams

(1768-1848)

Sixth President of the United States

Term of Office: March 4, 1825-March 3, 1829
First Lady: Louise Catherine Johnson
Vice President: John C. Calhoun

In 1801 the couple returned to Massachusetts, and Adams won a seat in the state senate before being elected to fill a vacant seat in the United States Senate. In 1807 he broke with the Federalist Party and supported President Jefferson's trade embargo. Adams later served as minister to Russia and as secretary of state for James Monroe. In the presidential election of 1824 Adams ran a strong second to Andrew Jackson in the electoral vote, but since no candidate had won an absolute majority, the House of Representatives elected the new president, and Adams won the decision.

As president, Adams attempted to pursue a program of national improvements, especially the creation of highways and canals that would link the newly developing western states with the rest of the country. But he was constantly embroiled in the perennial issue of tariffs – New Englanders demanding higher tariffs and Southerners demanding lower – and his efforts to cope with this growing sectionalism left him both frustrated and exhausted. Once he remarked that he could "scarcely conceive a more harassing, wearying, teasing condition of existence" than being president, and he was actually relieved when he lost the 1828 election outright to Andrew Jackson.

Adams returned to Braintree, where people urged him to return to Washington, this time as a member of the House of Representatives. Adams did run for office, was elected in 1831, and served in Washington until his death in 1848. In Congress he fought for the Bank of the United States, which was threatened by President Jackson, and supported the idea that the federal government had the right to free slaves in a period of war. In general, he found he liked being a legislator: he could both care for the needs of his constituents and speak out on important issues. On February 21, 1848, he suffered a stroke while working at his desk. He was brought to the room of the Speaker of the House, where he died two days later.

John Quincy Adams was a highly intelligent man who was perhaps better suited temperamentally to be a diplomat or a legislator than president. His diplomatic and political careers were broad and extensive, but he seemed happiest as a member of the House of Representatives, following his term as president.

He was born in Braintree, Massachusetts, in 1768, son of John Adams, the second president. John Quincy accompanied his father on a diplomatic mission to Europe in 1778, and, after living in Paris, Amsterdam, and Leyden, and eventually serving as his father's personal secretary, John Quincy returned to the United States and was graduated from Harvard University in 1787. Adams was appointed minister to the Netherlands in 1794 and there met his future wife, Louise Catherine Johnson, the daughter of another American diplomat. The couple married in 1797 and soon thereafter left for Berlin, where Adams was to serve as minister to Prussia.

Right: John Quincy Adams suffers a fatal stroke while in the U.S. House of Representatives in 1848. He was the only American to serve in Congress after having been president.

Andrew Jackson

(1767-1845)

Seventh President
of the United States

Term of Office: March 4, 1829-March 4, 1837
First Lady: Rachel Donelson Robards (died 1828)
Vice Presidents: John C. Calhoun, Martin Van Buren

I n his life and career Andrew Jackson personified the populist spirit of the American people. Jackson's two terms in office ended the period in which every president came either from Virginia or Massachusetts. Jackson was a frontiersman and fighter, a law-breaker as well as lawmaker. He was highly intelligent and complex, and he brought a vigor and forcefulness to the presidency that profoundly transformed its character.

Jackson was the first president to be raised in a log cabin. The building was situated in Waxhaws settlement on the border of North and South Carolina, and Jackson was born there on March 15,

1767, the third child of immigrants from Northern Ireland. His father died just before Jackson was born. From his early school days, Jackson was known as a "scrapper" who would fight anyone who insulted him on any occasion.

In 1780 Andrew and his older brother Robert joined the mounted militia of South Carolina. The brothers were captured by British soldiers, whereupon a British officer ordered Andrew to clean his boots. Andrew refused, claiming that he was a prisoner, not a servant. Enraged, the officer raised his sword and struck Andrew on his hand and head, leaving scars that lasted for life. Jackson and his brother were freed in a prisoner exchange, but shortly afterward, the boys' mother died, leaving Andrew an orphan at the age of 14. He soon showed his fortitude in the face of adversity.

After teaching school briefly Jackson studied the law and moved to Tennessee, where he met and married Rachel Donelson Robards in 1791. Later, in 1794, the couple was chagrined to learn that Rachel's divorce from her former husband had not become final until after the marriage. Therefore, in 1794, the couple re-married. This embarrassing episode remained with the Jacksons for many years and was used against Andrew when he campaigned for president. The couple had no children, but in 1809 they adopted the nephew of Mrs. Jackson.

Jackson served as a delegate to the Tennessee constitutional convention and in the United States House of Representatives in 1796-97. He later served effectively as a justice of the supreme court of Tennessee between 1798 and 1804, but his personal life remained stormy. He fought several duels and in 1806 killed Charles Dickinson, a lawyer, who had insulted Rachel Jackson.

In the War of 1812 Jackson became a national hero by defeating first the Creek Indians and then, at the Battle of New Orleans on January 8, 1815, the British army. Firing from behind earthworks, American militiamen shot down nearly 2000 British soldiers in under 20 minutes of fighting. American losses were only 14 men killed, 39 wounded, and 18 captured. It was the most one-sided victory so far gained by American troops.

In 1824 Jackson won a plurality of the popular vote and the electoral vote, but lost a runoff of the presidential election to John Quincy Adams. Jackson ran again in 1828; he defeated Adams handily but suffered a tragedy when Rachel Jackson died of a heart attack on December 22, 1828. Jackson became convinced that politically directed slights against Rachel regarding their marriage and re-marriage had killed her.

After taking office in 1829 Jackson brought the "spoils system" to a new level, replacing many of Adams' former officials with his own people. Yet he remained popular with the majority of Americans, for they saw in him not an Eastern aristocrat but one of their own. He initiated an aggressive policy against the Indian tribes and worked to remove many of them to west of the Mississippi River. Although this was typical of his generally ruthless behavior, Jackson was also capable of acts of great kindness. Indeed, he was inconsistent in many things, allowing that the president could not interfere with the policy of the state of Georgia toward the Cherokee nation, while maintaining that South Carolina must remain in

Left: Rachel Jackson. The president believed that her death from a heart attack in 1828 was the result of slurs made on her character during the presidential campaign of that year.

Below: Jackson at the Battle of New Orleans in 1815. It was the greatest U.S. victory of the War of 1812, but in the battle neither side realized that a peace treaty already had been signed by the negotiators in Ghent.

the Union and could not resist the high tariffs which had been created. This latter policy led to a major crisis in 1832. Jackson had just won re-election with a large majority when South Carolina declared that the tariff laws of 1828 and 1832 were null and void. South Carolina threatened to secede from the Union if federal duties were collected in Charleston. Jackson reacted swiftly and forcefully, sending troops and ships to converge on Charleston and obtaining authorization from the Congress to use force if necessary. A compromise tariff was pushed through and conflict was narrowly averted, but this "Nullification Crisis" was an ominous foreshadowing of the Civil War to come.

Jackson also attacked the Bank of the United States (which he saw as an undemocratic institution), withdrawing government funds from the bank and thereby depriving it of its former power. In 1837, on his last day in office, Jackson also established diplomatic relations with the new Republic of Texas, one of a succession of steps that would eventually lead to war with Mexico.

After retiring to Tennessee, Jackson died on June 8, 1845. For better or worse he had changed the American presidency into a vastly more powerful and personal office.

Left: President-elect Andrew Jackson pauses to speak to a crowd of well-wishers during his trip to Washington for his inauguration in 1829.

Below: George Catlin's portrait of the Seminole chief Osceola, who led his tribe into armed revolt rather than submit to Jackson's resettlement policies.

Martin Van Buren

(1782-1862)

Eighth President
of the United States

Term of Office: March 4, 1837-March 4, 1841
First Lady: None, wife died 1819
Vice President: Richard M. Johnson

Van Buren served as vice president during Jackson's second term, and Jackson made it clear that Van Buren was his choice for president in 1836.

Van Buren defeated William Henry Harrison in the election and was inaugurated on March 4, 1837. In his inauguration speech he announced his desire to follow in the wake of Jackson, his "illustrious predecessor." However, the new president was soon confronted by the Panic of 1837, which was the first full-scale depression the United States had faced. It was partly due to expansion following the opening of the Erie Canal in 1825 and to the subsequent extension of credit and loans for road and canal building. Van Buren recommended only the creation of an independent federal treasury, which would be safe from bank failures, to pay the federal government's obligations. But there was no provision for helping the people of the country in such a crisis, for Van Buren was essentially a Jeffersonian president, one who believed in limited government. Congressional opponents denounced Van Buren, and his popularity among the people suffered greatly. It is perhaps to his credit that Van Buren stuck to his principles despite opposition. Certainly he was not a sly rogue who would do anything that was politically expedient, as some of his foes claimed.

Van Buren lost to William Henry Harrison in the election of 1840, and although he ran again in 1848, Van Buren essentially retired to Kinderhook, New York, where he died on July 24, 1862.

Right: By the time of the 1840 election Van Buren's popularity had eroded badly, and he was easily defeated by Harrison.

Martin Van Buren was an elegant, sophisticated politician who was misunderstood by the American people. He ran for president three times but was elected only once, in 1836. He was born in Kinderhook, New York, on December 5, 1782, the descendant of Dutch emigrants to America. After practicing law and serving as a member of the New York legislature, Van Buren went to Washington in 1821 as a Senator. He was re-elected in 1827 and stood out as a leader of the anti-John Quincy Adams group in the Senate. In 1828 Van Buren won the governor's race in New York but soon resigned in order to serve as secretary of state for President Andrew Jackson. Although they were temperamental opposites, Jackson and Van Buren developed mutual liking.

William Henry Harrison

(1773-1841)

Ninth President
of the United States

Term of Office: March 4, 1841-April 4, 1841
First Lady: Anna Symmes
Vice President: John Tyler

In 1811 he won an important victory over Indians led by the Shawnee chief Tecumseh at the Battle of Tippecanoe. After serving as a general in the War of 1812, Harrison became a United States Senator from Ohio and also served as United States minister to Colombia in 1828.

Harrison ran for president in 1836 but was defeated by Martin Van Buren. In 1840 the two politicians ran against each other again, and this time Harrison led the Whig party to victory. He did so without declaring any particular campaign platform; instead, his campaign emphasized platitudes and slogans such as "Tippecanoe and Tyler too!" (Harrison's supporters even suggested that he was a frontiersman by birth, which was completely untrue.) In the election Harrison won narrowly in the popular vote but swept the electoral vote. At 68 he was the oldest man to be elected president. Unfortunately, he caught a bad cold on the rainy inaugural day, and, to the shock and surprise of the country, this Virginian patrician-turned frontier governor and Indian-fighter, died on April 4, 1841, just one month after becoming the nation's ninth president.

Right above: Harrison's election propaganda stressed his military exploits and the fact that he had been born in a log cabin (which was wholly untrue).

Right below: An artist's version of one of the encounters between the Shawnee chief Tecumseh and Benjamin Harrison.

William Henry Harrison was another Virginian who became president. Born on February 9, 1773, in Charles City County, Virginia, Harrison came from a notable family – his father had served in the Continental Congress and had signed the Declaration of Independence. Harrison's military and political career led to a climax of the presidency, but Harrison served as president only for one month before his untimely death.

Harrison had originally planned to study medicine, but he entered the army after his father died in 1791. He married Anna Symmes in 1795, and the couple had six sons and four daughters. In 1798 President Adams named Harrison secretary of the Northwest Territory, and in 1800 Harrison became governor of the Indiana Territory. Holding that post for 12 years, Harrison became well-known for his efforts to make treaties with Indians, and then for his vigor in fighting the Indians when war came.

John Tyler

(1790-1862)

Tenth President
of the United States

Term of Office: April 6, 1841-March 4, 1845
First Lady: Letitia Christian, died while Tyler was in office
Vice President: None

Right: Tyler was swept into the vice presidency on the strength of the razzle-dazzle campaign mounted for Harrison in 1840. Within a single month fate had elevated Tyler to the presidency.

J ohn Tyler was the first vice president to replace a president who had died in office. During his presidency Tyler had several sharp quarrels both with the opposition Democrats and with his own Whig Party. Although denounced by the press of his day, Tyler has been praised by later historians for his independent convictions.

Tyler was born on March 29, 1790, in Charles City County, Virginia. His father was, at times, governor of Virginia, speaker of the Virginia House of Delegates, and a judge. Tyler was graduated from William and Mary at 17 and was elected to the House of Delegates at 21 and the United States House of Representatives at 26. Tyler became known as an advocate of strict interpretation of the Constitution, in the tradition of Thomas Jefferson. An ardent supporter of states rights, in 1832 he resigned from Congress and from the Democratic Party which had backed President Jackson in the nullification crisis of that year.

In 1840 Tyler was nominated for vice president by the Whig Party, and, following the untimely death of William Henry Harrison, Tyler was sworn in as the tenth president. When the Congress, led by arch-Whig Henry Clay, called for higher tariffs and a Bank of the United States, Tyler vetoed the bills that came to his desk. He was strongly criticized for this, and he endured more censure when, at Clay's prompting, his entire Cabinet – with the exception of Daniel Webster – resigned in protest of his vetoes. Later in his term Congress even considered impeachment resolutions, but these were defeated.

Tyler is best remembered for signing bills which admitted Texas and Florida into the Union. In his retirement Tyler served as a member of a peace commission seeking compromise between the North and the South in early 1861. He died a year later, on January 18, 1862.

James Knox Polk

(1795-1849)

Eleventh President
of the United States

Term of Office: March 4, 1845-March 4, 1849
First Lady: Sarah Childress
Vice President: George M. Dallas

Beginning in 1825, Polk served seven consecutive terms in the United States House of Representatives. He was a loyal Democrat and a tireless worker, missing only one day in Congress during 14 years. He later served as governor of Tennessee, where he declared his stands for states' rights and slavery. Then, in 1844 Polk became a surprise nominee for the presidency.

Former President Martin Van Buren was the frontrunner for the Democratic nomination, but he could not secure enough delegates during the balloting at the party convention. After the eighth ballot Massachusetts historian George Bancroft nominated Polk, who was unanimously accepted on the next ballot. Thus Polk became the first political "dark horse" in American history to be nominated for the presidency.

Polk stood for annexation of Texas, and occupation of the Oregon Territory, which was disputed with Great Britain. His memorable campaign slogan was "Fifty-Four Forty or Fight," referring to an American Oregon up to the latitude of 54° 40'. Polk narrowly defeated Henry Clay in the election of 1844 and was inaugurated on March 4, 1845.

Polk soon entered into negotiations with the British for a compromise on the Oregon question and eventually settled on a boundary at 40°N. He also established a new independent treasury (as Martin Van Buren had done before him) and reduced the tariff, which helped Southern states more than it did Northern markets. But his largest legacy to the country was undoubtedly the huge territorial acquisition of all or parts of present-day Arizona, California, Colorado, Nevada, New Mexico, Utah, and Wyoming that resulted from the Mexican War.

The principal cause of the war was the United States' decision to bow to the wishes of the Texans to be annexed: the Texans claimed that Texas was a sovereign republic, but Mexico insisted that it

Right: In the beginning of the final phase of the Mexican War, U.S. troops come on shore at Vera Cruz on March 9, 1847. As a result of this war Polk was able to add more territory to the United States than any president save Jefferson.

James Knox Polk was one of the more successful presidents. During his single presidential term he acquired large amounts of territory, faced down Great Britain, reduced the tariff, and established a new, independent treasury. Worn-out from his efforts, Polk died less than a year after leaving the White House.

Polk was born on November 2, 1795, near Pineville, North Carolina, the oldest of ten children of Irish immigrants. He was graduated from the University of North Carolina in 1818 and practiced law in Tennessee. He married Sarah Childress in 1824; the couple had no children.

Above: At the climax of the Mexican War, U.S. troops storm Mexico City on September 14, 1847.

was still a Mexican province. After failing to buy off the Mexicans, Polk, early in 1846, sent General Zachary Taylor with 4000 soldiers to occupy the disputed territory. When the Mexicans resisted, Polk went to Congress and asked for a declaration of war, stating that Mexico had "shed American blood on American soil."

The course of the war was rapid. Time and again Mexican forces proved unable to face the American army effectively. There were protests against the war in the United States, but Polk over-

rode all objections, and by 1848 the war was over and the United States was larger by some 500,000 square miles.

In 1848 Polk deliberately chose not to seek re-election. He retired to Nashville, Tennessee, where he died on June 15, 1849. It had been a short presidency, and though his motives and means may have been questionable on moral grounds, there can be no doubt that according to Polk's lights his had been an immensely successful and praiseworthy administration.

Zachary Taylor

(1784-1850)

Twelfth President
of the United States

Term of Office: March 5, 1849-July 9, 1850
First Lady: Margaret Smith
Vice President: Millard Fillmore

Mexican War general that Taylor is best known. In 1846 Taylor led 4000 men to the disputed border between Mexico and the United States, as instructed by President Polk. Mexican cavalry crossed the Rio Grande River and skirmished with Taylor's men. Taylor defended his position and won the subsequent battles of Palo Alto and Resaca de la Palma, as well as capturing the Mexican towns of Matamoros and Monterrey. In February, 1847, Taylor's 5000-man army was attacked at Buena Vista by a Mexican force three times as large under the leadership of General Santa Anna, yet Taylor and his men withstood several assaults and eventually won the battle. This victory confirmed Taylor as a war hero and led to his nomination and election in 1848, the first national election to be held at the same time in all of the different states. As president, Taylor pondered plans for a canal across Nicaragua and faced a difficult choice as to whether California and New Mexico should be admitted into the Union as slave states or free states. He had vowed to hold the Union together by force if necessary, but he died of cholera on July 9, 1850, just as the Congressional debates were getting under way.

Right above: An anti-Taylor political cartoon accuses him of having been a butcher in the Mexican War.

Right below: President Zachary Taylor.

Zachary Taylor served as president for one year, and his hold upon the memory of the American people is strongest because of his military career. "Old Rough and Ready," as he was called, never lost a battle.

Taylor was born near Barboursville, Virginia, on November 24, 1784, the third son in a family of nine children. His father had been an officer in the Revolutionary War, and Taylor himself became a lieutenant in 1808 and slowly rose through the ranks. In the War of 1812 he successfully defended Fort Harrison against the British. In 1832 Taylor received the surrender of Chief Black Hawk, thus ending the Black Hawk War. Taylor also defeated the Seminole Indians of Florida, but it is as a

Millard Fillmore

(1800-1874)

Thirteenth President
of the United States

Term of Office: July 10, 1850-March 3, 1853
First Lady: Abigail Powers
Vice President: None

Taylor died on July 9, 1850, and Fillmore was sworn in the following day. Faced with the Congressional debate over the status of the territories of California and New Mexico, Fillmore favored the set of laws which became known as the Compromise of 1850. The legislation admitted California as a free state and created territorial governments for Utah and New Mexico. Though the Compromise abolished the slave trade in the District of Columbia, it also created a strong fugitive slave law. This patchwork legislation temporarily averted a rupture in the Union, but the issue was not clearly solved and would resurface by the mid 1850s. Fillmore's presidency was also known for economic and internal improvements and for the mission of Commodore Perry to Japan.

Fillmore lost the Whig nomination in 1852, and although he sought the presidency again in 1856, he came in third in that election, ending his political career. Abigail Fillmore died in 1853, and in 1858 Fillmore married a widow, Caroline McIntosh. Fillmore himself died on March 8, 1874.

Right above: A Japanese artist's impression of a Western warship like the one on which Perry made his historic visit.

Right below: A view of San Francisco. Whether California would enter the Union slave or free was a major issue in Filmore's presidency.

Born to a poor family in Locke, New York, on January 7, 1800, Fillmore was apprenticed to a cloth-maker at the age of 14 and later bought his freedom for $30. Almost entirely self-educated, Fillmore profited by his marriage to Abigail Powers in 1826, for she helped his social standing and brought him needed connections. The couple moved to Albany when Fillmore entered the state assembly. Later, Fillmore served in Congress as a Whig, lost the New York governor's race in 1844, and then served as the state's comptroller-general before being nominated for vice president under Zachary Taylor in 1848.

Franklin Pierce

(1804-1869)

Fourteenth President of the United States

Term of Office: March 4, 1853-March 4, 1857
First Lady: Jane Means Appleton
Vice President: William R.D. King

1833. In 1837 he became the youngest member of the United States Senate. In 1834 he had married Jane Means Appleton, and, because his wife suffered from tuberculosis, Pierce resigned from the Senate in 1842.

He served as a brigadier general in the Mexican War and participated in the final march to Mexico City. In 1852 Pierce was nominated for the presidency after the Democratic convention had gone through 49 ballots. Pierce then went on to defeat his former military commander, General Winfield Scott, in the election and was inaugurated on March 4, 1853. One of his sons had just been killed in a railway accident, and Mrs. Pierce was overcome with grief; she remained in mourning and did not greatly participate in the role of First Lady.

Pierce's presidency came at a time of great prosperity, and the first trade treaty with newly-opened Japan was concluded in 1854. Politically, however, the country was deeply divided over the issue of whether the Union should permit slavery to exist in new states. Pierce signed the Kansas-Nebraska Act, allowing the residents of the territories to decide for themselves whether their states would be "slave" or "free." Predictably, this satisfied none of the extremists on either side of the issue.

Following his return to private life Pierce and his wife traveled abroad in an attempt to improve Mrs. Pierce's health, but she died in 1863. During the Civil War, Pierce criticized Lincoln for taking the nation into the conflict. Pierce died on December 8, 1869, and was buried in Concord, New Hampshire.

F ranklin Pierce governed the United States during one of the nation's most prosperous times, the mid-1850s. However, storm clouds that foreshadowed the Civil War were present, and Pierce endured a personal tragedy while he was in office.

Pierce was born on November 23, 1804, in Hillsboro, New Hampshire, the seventh of nine children. His father had been a militia general in the Revolution and also the governor of New Hampshire. Pierce was graduated from Bowdoin College and opened his own law office in Concord, New Hampshire, before becoming a Congressman in

Right: Rare daguerreotype of Franklin Pierce.

James Buchanan

(1791-1868)

Fifteenth President of the United States

Term of Office: March 4, 1857-March 3, 1861
First Lady: None
Vice President: John C. Breckenridge

was the only president who never married; a traumatic early love affair may indeed have pushed him into politics as a means of escape. He was Polk's secretary of state during the Mexican War and also served as President Franklin Pierce's minister to Great Britain.

Buchanan won the 1856 presidential election by only a plurality of the popular vote but with a clear majority in the Electoral College. Although he personally opposed slavery, he doubted whether the federal government had any right to impose its will on individual states. Northern Democrats charged that Buchanan favored the South in the controversy over whether Kansas should be slave or free, and Buchanan thus found himself at odds with Congress and was unable to put through his own agenda in domestic policy. When Buchanan left office in 1861 his popularity was low, and he became a national scapegoat during the Civil War. Buchanan supported Lincoln during the war and managed to write his memoirs before he died on June 1, 1868.

J ames Buchanan enjoyed a distinguished career as a diplomat and legislator before becoming president. Once in office, he was unable to prevent regionalism and the politics of slavery from bringing the Union to a crisis point. By the time he left office in 1861 several Southern states had seceded, and the Civil War was about to begin.

Buchanan was born on April 23, 1791, near Mercersburg, Pennsylvania, the second of 11 children. He was graduated from Dickinson College, studied law, and then started his own law practice. He served as a Congressman and Senator, as well as minister to Russia from 1832 to 1834. Buchanan

Right: Harriet Lane, Buchanan's niece, acted as official hostess for the celibate president.

Abraham Lincoln

(1809-1865)

Sixteenth President of the United States

Term of Office: March 4, 1861-April 15, 1865
First Lady: Mary Todd
Vice Presidents: Hannibal Hamlin, Andrew Johnson

February 12, 1809, Lincoln was taken from his native Kentucky in 1816 when his family moved to the frontier in Indiana. Lincoln had only one year of schooling and worked splitting rails and logs to help support his family. In 1831 he made his way to New Salem, Illinois, where he had several varied and unsuccessful careers. In 1832 he volunteered to serve in the Black Hawk War. Although he saw no action, Lincoln was elected captain by his fellow militiamen, an early indication of his ability to lead and motivate people.

In 1834 Lincoln was elected to the Indiana legislature. His skill in debate was admired, and he obtained a reputation for complete honesty and trustworthiness. He studied law on his own and received a law license in 1836. Only five years after leaving his family, Lincoln had won success both as a politician and a lawyer. In 1842 he married Mary Todd, and the couple eventually had four children, all boys.

Lincoln won election to the United States House of Representatives in 1846, and in the early 1850s he became known as an opponent of the Kansas-Nebraska Act, which would allow new territories to decide whether they would allow slavery or not. Lincoln had been a member of the Whig Party, but in 1856 he joined the newly-formed Republican Party, which was known for its anti-slavery stand. The famous Lincoln-Douglas debates occurred in 1858: between August and October, Lincoln and

Right: This photograph of Mary Todd Lincoln in a ball gown was taken around 1861.

The only question about Abraham Lincoln's presidency is not whether it was great but whether it was the greatest of all. He rose from humble, though not impoverished, beginnings to preside over the United States during the great crisis of the Civil War, and his self-developed powers of persuasion, reason, and persistence sustained the United States throughout that agonizing conflict.

Lincoln was the second of the three children of Thomas Lincoln and Nancy Hanks. Born on

THE UNION MUST AND SHALL BE PRESERVED

FREE SPEECH, FREE HOMES, FREE TERRITORY.

PROTECTION TO AMERICAN INDUSTRY

FOR PRESIDENT
ABRAHAM LINCOLN
OF ILLINOIS

FOR VICE PRESIDENT
HANNIBAL HAMLIN
OF MAINE

LITH.BY W.H.REASE

COR.4TH & CHESTNUT STs.PHILADA.

Above: A Republican poster for the election of 1860 – the election that was the proximate cause of the Civil War.

Senator Stephen Douglas debated the issue of slavery throughout Illinois, and the debates gave Lincoln national attention and allowed him to run for the Republican Party presidential nomination in 1860.

Lincoln won the nomination on the third ballot in Chicago and then faced three different opponents in the fall elections. Lincoln won less than half of the popular vote, but he won a majority of the electoral vote and thus became the first member of the Republican Party to become president. But the Southern states which had voted against Lincoln now began formally to secede from the Union, and by the date of Lincoln's inauguration, March 4, 1861, seven had already done so. Lincoln announced that he did not intend to destroy the institution of slavery but that he would do all that was necessary to hold the Union together. When Confederate General P.G.T. Beaureguard's artillery opened fire on Federal Fort Sumter in Charleston Harbor, Lincoln moved into action, calling for militia volunteers to put down the Southern rebellion.

In the spring and summer of 1861 Northerners expected a quick and easy fight, but their defeat in the battle of Bull Run in July showed that this would instead be a fight to the finish. One of Lincoln's greatest troubles lay in finding talented generals. Materially, the North enjoyed numerous advantages over the South, but the caliber of military leadership was at first far stronger in the South. In the first two years of the war commanders such as Lee, Jackson, and Bragg con-

sistently outfought Northern generals such as McClellan, Hooker, and Pope.

In the Northern states Lincoln also faced serious challenges. There were enormous riots against the draft in New York City, and Lincoln suspended the right of habeas corpus to areas in which there were known to be Southern sympathizers. Lincoln wisely worked to blockade the South by sea, but even there he faced potential trouble: Great Britain and the United States came close to war over the issue of U.S. interference with British trade with the Confederacy. Lincoln dealt with these and other problems with admirable wisdom and skill, but the stress took its toll; old photographs vividly record the difference in Lincoln's appearance before and during the Civil War. Never before or since has a United States president had to face so many direct or imminent situations that were potentially disastrous.

On January 1, 1863, Lincoln formally announced the Emancipation Proclamation, in which he declared that all slaves in the states that were in rebellion were thenceforth free. Lincoln did not include the District of Columbia or certain border states in this proclamation, probably because he wanted to ensure their continued support for his policies. Six months later the Union Army triumphed in the most decisive battle of the war, Gettysburg, and Lincoln subsequently went to the battlefield to deliver the single most famous speech in American history, the supremely eloquent Gettysburg Address.

By 1864 Lincoln had at last found the general he

Left: The First Battle of
Bull Run, July 21, 1861.
The Union defeat in this
first important
engagement between the
Northern and Southern
armies dispelled any
illusion that the war could
soon be ended.

Below: Lincoln confers
with General George B.
McClellan in the field
soon after the end of the
bloody Battle of Antietam
in 1862.

needed: Ulysses S. Grant, a man who had the iron will necessary to lead the Union Armies to victory. Lincoln would hear much criticism of Grant because of the huge casualties suffered in his advance on Richmond in 1864, but Lincoln always said "I can't spare this man, he fights."

In 1864 Lincoln faced another kind of challenge when he ran for re-election. One of his former generals, George B. McClellan, was his opponent. The contest looked undecided until some victories by the Union Armies late in the year turned the tide for Lincoln. He was inaugurated for the second time on March 4, 1865. His speech was a model of conciliation. He urged the nation to work together, "With kindness toward all, with malice towards none."

Confederate General Robert E. Lee surrendered on April 9 1865. The Civil War was at last over, but the man who had held the North together, who had defeated the South, and who was now ready to bind the nation together in a spirit of charity was not to see the fruits of his labors. On April 14, 1865, Lincoln was shot by actor John Wilkes Booth while the president was attending a performance of *Our American Cousin* at the Ford's Theatre in Washington. He died at 7:22 in the morning of the next day. His body was carried by train to Springfield, Illinois; all along the way huge crowds of people gathered to watch the passing of the train and to mourn the loss of the great president. Seldom in history has a man given so much to his country.

Andrew Johnson

(1808-1875)

Seventeenth President of the United States

Term of Office: April 15, 1865-March 3, 1869
First Lady: Eliza McCardle
Vice President: None

After being gerrymandered out of office, Johnson recovered so successfully that he won the governorship of Tennessee twice. On the advent of the Civil War in 1865 Johnson declared that he would fight for the Union and became in essence a United States Senator without a state. Lincoln put Johnson on his presidential ticket in 1864 in order to balance the ticket by including both a Northerner and Southerner as candidates.

On Inauguration Day, March 4, 1865, Vice President Johnson was ill. He drank some whiskey in order to bolster himself, but the result was a disastrous speech in which he rambled and ranted. It was an inauspicious beginning.

Following the assassination of Lincoln, Johnson was sworn in as president on April 15, 1865. The self-made Southerner was a strict constructionist, and he put relatively mild guidelines on what Southern states had to do in order to rejoin the Union. Because of this gentle approach, Johnson soon came to be regarded as a traitor to the Northern cause. Congressmen such as Thaddeus Stevens worked actively against Johnson and his program, and the Radical Republicans who dominated the Congress impeached Johnson in 1868 after he had removed the secretary of war. The final vote against Johnson failed by one vote, and he was able to serve out his term more quietly. Johnson retired to Tennessee and died on July 31, 1875.

Right: Ailing Senator Thaddeus Stevens reads to the Senate the draft of his resolution of impeachment that will bring President Johnson to trial.

Andrew Johnson was one of the most unfortunate of the presidents. His limited abilities as a conciliator were completely inadequate to cope with the harsh political climate after the Civil War. Misunderstood, Johnson was impeached and nearly removed from office.

Johnson was born on December 29, 1808, in Raleigh, North Carolina. His father had been a porter, and Johnson was briefly apprenticed to a tailor. Johnson relocated to Tennessee, and became involved in local politics as a town council member, mayor, member of the state legislature, and eventually as a member of Congress in 1843.

Ulysses Simpson Grant

(1822-1885)

Eighteenth President
of the United States

Term of Office: March 4, 1869-March 4, 1877
First Lady: Julia Boggs Dent
Vice Presidents: Schuyler Colfax, Henry Wilson

Right: During the Civil War, Grant was made a lieutenant general, the highest military rank awarded to any American since George Washington.

Americans remember Ulysses S. Grant best for his successful prosecution of the Civil War and his clemency when dealing with Lee's defeated Army at Appomatox Court House in 1865. Grant was in fact a better soldier than he was a president.

His original name was Hiram Ulysses Grant, but a bureaucratic error at West Point converted his name to Ulysses Simpson Grant, and he kept that name for the rest of his life. Born in Point Pleasant, Ohio, on April 27, 1822, Grant was not a very good student in school, and he did poorly in his father's tanning business. In the military he did better, serving with distinction in numerous battles in the Mexican War, although he was privately against the conflict. Grant married Julia Dent in 1848, and the couple subsequently had four children. Grant

was so miserable when Army duties kept him away from his family for two years that he resigned from the Army and tried farming and real-estate, at both of which he ultimately failed.

Grant volunteered at the start of the Civil War, and soon rose to high rank because of his bulldog determination to fight the enemy and hit the Confederacy where it hurt. Grant captured forts Donelson and Henry in 1862, Vicksburg in 1863, and in 1864 he became a lieutenant general and commander of all the Union armies. Grant fought Lee's Army of Nothern Virginia in an unrelenting, punishing campaign between 1864 and 1865, finally accepting Lee's surrender at Appomatox Court House on April 9, 1865.

Grant was elected president in 1868. He enjoyed great popular support, but he was not a good politician. He was in fact an extremely passive chief executive, with few specific programs or goals. Grant also made the mistake of appointing friends to high positions – friends who often betrayed his trust and abused their offices. Although he served two full terms, Grant's presidency was anti-climactic compared to his generalship in the war. Following his term of office, Grant retired to upstate New York, where he fell into poverty at one point and had to sell his swords as war souvenirs. Congress restored him to the rank of general and granted him a salary just months before he died, on July 23, 1885.

Rutherford Birchard Hayes

(1822-1893)

Nineteenth President
of the United States

Term of Office: March 4, 1877-March 3, 1881
First Lady: Lucy Ware Webb
Vice President: William A. Wheeler

war Hayes went to Washington as a member of the House of Representatives. His service there, combined with three terms as governor of Ohio, lifted Hayes to the Republican nomination in 1876. Samuel Tilden, Hayes's opponent, narrowly defeated Hayes in the popular vote, but came up one electoral vote shy of what he needed to win. Since the election process was deadlocked, Congress appointed an Electoral Commission which worked out a compromise in early March, 1877. Hayes became president, contingent on his promise to withdraw Federal troops from the Southern states and end Reconstruction. Hayes did both of these things promptly after his inauguration on March 4, 1877.

Hayes then tried to reform the civil service system but was unable to move his legislation through Congress. He was, however, successful in restoring public confidence in paper money by redeeming it with gold or silver. After he vacated the presidency in 1881 Hayes retired to private life, commenting that "nobody ever left the presidency with less regret . . . than I do." He died 12 years later, on January 17, 1893.

Right above: Democrat Samuel Tilden, loser to Hayes in the disputed election of 1876.

Right below: A cartoon depicting Hayes as the man who will at last reconcile the North and the South.

Rutherford B. Hayes became president under confused and controversial circumstances. He is best remembered for having ended the period of Reconstruction in the South and for the dignified and modest manner in which he and his wife ran the White House.

Hayes was born on October 4, 1822, in Delaware, Ohio. A champion speller in elementary school, he went on to Kenyon College and Harvard Law School before setting up his own law practice. He commanded a regiment of Ohio volunteers in the Civil War and saw much action – he was wounded four times. Immediately after the

James Abram Garfield

(1831-1881)

Twentieth President of the United States

Term of Office: March 4, 1881-September 19, 1881
First Lady: Lucretia Rudolph
Vice President: Chester A. Arthur

In 1880 Garfield was nominated by the Republican Party on the 36th ballot. He had not been the favorite candidate, but the party was deadlocked between the "Half-Breeds," who favored James G. Blaine, and the "Stalwarts," who favored Ulysses Grant. Once in office, Garfield promoted a number of Half-Breed Republicans to the civil service, thereby enraging many Stalwarts. At the height of these passions over patronage, on July 2, 1881, Garfield was shot twice in a railroad station as he was leaving Washington on a trip to Williams College. The assassin, Charles Giuteau, cried out, "I am a Stalwart, and [Vice President] Arthur is president now!" Guiteau was distraught because he had not received a diplomatic post that he wanted: the issue of civil service reform could not be left half-attended any longer. Garfield survived his wounds only until September 19, 1881, retaining all the powers of the presidency until his death.

FRANK LESLIE'S ILLUSTRATED NEWSPAPER

No. 1,316—Vol. LII   NEW YORK, JULY 16, 1881.   [Price 10 Cents.

James Garfield held office for only a short time, and his assassination brought to the fore problems that were festering in the United States – the need for civil service reform and bitter antagonisms within the Republican Party.

Garfield was born on November 19, 1831, in Orange, Ohio, the youngest of five children. He attended Hiram College, then Williams College, and then returned to Hiram College, where he was first a professor and then the college president. In the Civil War he served as a colonel of Ohio volunteers, seeing action in several battles and winning distinction at the battle of Chickamagua in 1863. In 1862, while still in the army, he was elected to the House of Representatives, beginning his political career. He served nine terms in the House and was a member of the Electoral Commission which ruled on the disputed 1876 election.

Right above: Garfield and his daughter.

Right below: Garfield's assassiation.

Chester Alan Arthur

(1829-1886)

Twenty-first President
of the United States

Term of Office: September 20, 1881-March 4, 1885
First Lady: Ellen Lewis Herndon, died 1880, before Arthur's term began
Vice President: None

and studying law. During the Civil War, Arthur served as the inspector-general for the New York militia forces. In 1871 he became the collector of the New York Custom House, which had over 1000 employees. In this position he became so notorious as a dispenser of patronage jobs that in 1878 President Hayes suspended him. Apparently unchastened, the versatile Arthur went on to become the head of the party machine in New York City. In 1880 he became the choice for Republican vice-presidential nominee by those "Stalwarts" who had wanted Ulysses S. Grant to run once more. Following Garfield's death, Arthur became president on September 20, 1881.

As president, Arthur strove to rise above partisanship. He signed the Pendleton Civil Service Act, which created a bipartisan Civil Service Commission, classifications of all federal jobs and competitive examinations to fill those positions. Arthur also had several sharp confrontations with his own party faction Congress, often over patronage-related issues, and this cost him renomination in 1884. He retired to New York, where he died of Bright's Disease on November 18, 1886.

Right above: A Mathew Brady photograph taken of Arthur while he was on a fishing trip.

Right below: President Arthur registering to vote in New York City.

Chester A. Arthur was considered unlikely to be an effective president. He was deeply involved in rough-and-tumble state politics and had even once been suspended from an important position by President Hayes. But Arthur was less predictable than people assumed. The civil service was reformed during his administration, and he fought the potentially corrupting practice of patronage with surprising vigor.

Arthur was born in Fairfield, Vermont, on October 5, 1829. He attended Union College in Schenectady, New York, before teaching school

Grover Cleveland

(1837-1908)

Twenty-second and Twenty-fourth President of the United States

Terms of Office: March 4, 1885-March 4, 1889. March 4, 1893-March 4, 1897
First Lady: Frances Folsom
Vice Presidents: Thomas A. Hendricks, Adlai E. Stevenson

Right: A Frederick Opper cartoon called "The Sea Serpent Season" pokes fun at rumors about a third term for Cleveland.

Grover Cleveland seldom hesitated to use his presidential veto power, yet he believed in a "laissez-faire" government which intervened only to protect individual liberties. Cleveland saw his role as that of a watchdog who opposed favoritism in all its forms.

He was born in Caldwell, New Jersey, on March 18, 1837, the fifth of nine children of a Presbyterian minister. Cleveland grew up in western New York and moved to the Buffalo area after his father died in 1853. An uncle placed him in a Buffalo law office, and Cleveland began to experiment with his interest in politics – serving first as a Democratic ward-worker and then as sheriff of Erie County. He won the mayoral election in Buffalo in 1881 and

then the gubernatorial election in 1882. Famous for his integrity, Cleveland was known as a veto governor because of his efforts to thwart corruption and patronage.

He was popular with businessmen of both parties, thanks to his staunch support of free enterprise, and this helped him to be nominated for the presidency by the Democrats in 1884. He won the election by a narrow margin of 29,000 votes, ending 24 years of Republicans in the White House. In 1886 Cleveland married Frances Folsom (his 21-year old bride became the youngest of all First Ladies), and the couple had five children.

Cleveland was forced by his own party to replace many Republican civil servants with Democrats, but he defended executive privilege when Republican Senators tried to require him to release all information regarding political dismissals. Cleveland approved numerous Civil War veterans' pension bills, but he vetoed hundreds of others – actions which took considerable political courage. He also attacked the high tariff beloved of businessmen and was therefore not unduly surprised when he lost the 1888 election to Benjamin Harrison. Between 1889 and 1892 Cleveland worked as a lawyer in New York City, but his political eclipse ended with his comeback-election in 1892. Cleveland thus became the only president ever to serve two nonconsecutive terms.

His second term was marred by a severe economic depression in which some 4,000,000 Americans were out of work. Cleveland failed to obtain the tariff reform that he wanted, and he lost popularity through events such as the Pullman Strike, in which he sent federal soldiers to Chicago to restore railroad and mail operations. But Cleveland did enjoy one notable diplomatic victory. In 1895 he obtained from Congress the authority to determine the correct boundary between Venezeula and British Guiana. When Great Britain eventually submitted to United States arbitration, it became clear that the United States was, in the words of Cleveland's secretary of state, "practically sovereign on this continent."

Following his second term, Cleveland retired to Princeton, New Jersey. He lectured and wrote extensively until his death on June 24, 1908.

Benjamin Harrison

(1833-1901)

Twenty-third President of the United States

Term of Office: March 4, 1889-March 3, 1893
First Lady: Caroline Lavinia Scott
Vice President: Levi P. Morton

Right above: An Opper cartoon depicts Harrison as a microbe.

Right below: A formal photographic portrait of President Harrison.

Benjamin Harrison was the only president whose grandfather had preceeded him in that office. Born on August 20, 1833, in North Bend, Ohio, Harrison attended Farmers' College in Cincinnati and was graduated from Miami University in Oxford, Ohio, before reading law and working as the city attorney for Indianapolis. He later became the reporter for the state supreme court and taught Sunday school in his free time.

During the Civil War, Harrison served as a colonel of Indiana volunteers and was promoted to brigadier-general in 1865. After again working as a lawyer, Harrison was elected to the United States Senate in 1881. In the following year the Republican Party nominated Harrison for the presidency on the strength of his pro-business policies, his war record, and his popularity with Civil War veterans. Harrison lost the popular vote to Grover Cleveland but won in the Electoral College, with 233 votes to Cleveland's 168.

Harrison was known for his support of high tariffs that favored business, but his administration also instituted the Sherman Anti-Trust Act that outlawed trusts and monopolies which hindered trade. In 1890 the Democrats regained control of the House of Representatives, and some of them expressed discontent regarding the size of Harrison's national budget – nearly a billion dollars! The Speaker of the House retorted that, "This is a billion dollar country!" It was indeed a time of industrial and economic growth.

Harrison was defeated in his 1892 bid for re-election by Grover Cleveland. Harrison's wife had died in October, 1892, two weeks before the election. Harrison returned to Indianapolis and practiced law until his death on March 13, 1901.

43

William McKinley

(1843-1901)

Twenty-fifth President
of the United States

Term of Office: March 4, 1897-September 14, 1901
First Lady: Ida Saxton
Vice Presidents: Garret A. Hobart, Theodore Roosevelt

prosecuting attorney, all the while supporting the political career of his former military commander, Rutherford B. Hayes.

McKinley was elected to the House of Representatives in 1876 and served there from 1877 to 1891, with a short break during 1884-85. He became nationally known as a spokesman for tariff protection for American goods, and he sponsored the McKinley Tarrif Act of 1890. He had married Ida Saxton in 1871; following the early deaths of their two daughters, Mrs McKinley became virtually an invalid.

Following two terms as governor of Ohio, and an unsuccessful run for the Republican nomination in 1892, McKinley was nominated and elected in 1896. His campaign had emphasized tariff protection and support of the gold standard, but McKinley's time in office was largely absorbed by foreign affairs. In 1898 anti-Spanish feeling was running high in the United States as the newspapers called for American intervention in the Cuban revolt against Spanish colonial rule. McKinley sought a diplomatic solution but was virtually forced into asking Congress for a declaration of war when the explosion and sinking of U.S.S. *Maine* in Havana harbor in February, 1898, was popularly attributed to Spanish sabotage.

The war was swift and victorious, demonstrating American naval and military power to the world. At the treaty of Paris in 1899 the United States received Puerto Rico, Guam, and the Phillipines. McKinley also annexed Hawaii and occupied Wake Island. Later, during the Chinese Boxer Rebellion, McKinley sent 5000 American soldiers to serve as part of an international military force to protect foreigners in China.

In domestic affairs, McKinley supported both the high Dingley Tariff of 1897 and the Gold Standard Act of 1900, which made the gold dollar the only standard for currency. McKinley was re-elected in 1900, and he seemed ready to enjoy a triumphant second term, for nearly all of his initial goals had been accomplished. But on September 6, 1901, McKinley was shot by an assassin named Leon Czolgosz, at the Pan-American Exposition in Buffalo, New York. McKinley died on September 14, 1901, leaving the presidency to his vice president, Theodore Roosevelt.

William McKinley was elected on a domestic affairs platform but spent most of his presidency dealing with foreign policy. The last Civil War veteran to be elected president, McKinley led the United States into its only significant flirtation with old-fashioned imperialism.

McKinley was born on January 29, 1843, in Niles, Ohio, the seventh of nine children of working-class parents. He attended Allegheny College and enlisted in the Civil War as a private in the Ohio infantry, rising to the rank of brevet major by the war's conclusion. He then read the law, was admitted to the Ohio bar, and served as a county

Right: An Opper cartoon shows a weeping nurse McKinley taking care of baby "Gold Standard" for political reasons, while neglecting his own darling, "Protectionism."

Theodore Roosevelt

(1858-1919)

Twenty-sixth President of the United States

Term of Office: September 14, 1901-March 3, 1909
First Lady: Edith Kermit Carow
Vice President: Charles W. Fairbanks

Right: A young Teddy Roosevelt (1885) poses in buckskins.

Theodore Roosevelt was one of the most energetic and engaging of the presidents of the United States. He mixed politics and personality to a degree rarely seen in national leaders. Like the country he served, Roosevelt was a mix of liberal and conservative. The same man who backed certain labor unions in their strikes also promoted a revolution in Panama in order to pave the way for his greatest single project, the Canal that joined the Atlantic and Pacific Ocean fleets of the United States Navy.

Roosevelt was born on October 27, 1858, in New York City. As a child he suffered from both asthma and astigmatism, but far from causing him to become sedentary or retiring, these handicaps instead prompted the young Roosevelt to pursue the "strenuous life" – hiking, camping, cattle-ranching, and big-game hunting. Roosevelt was graduated from Harvard in 1880 and married Alice Hathaway Lee on his twenty-second birthday. In February, 1884, he suffered a double personal tragedy when his wife and his mother died on the same day, the former of complications from child-birth and the latter of typhoid fever.

Roosevelt resigned from the New York state assembly, to which he had been elected three years earlier, and went west to run two cattle ranches in the Dakota Territory. In 1886 he married Edith Kermit Carow, and the couple eventually had five children. His political career now began to develop at a rapid pace; he became a member of the Civil Service Commission and president of the Board of Police Commissioners in New York City, and in 1897 President McKinley appointed him assistant secretary of the navy. Roosevelt delighted in this last position – he was a great believer in the primacy of naval power and had written a book on the naval war of 1812. As sentiment for war with Spain grew, the aggressive Roosevelt became impatient with McKinley's temporizing and privately criticized the president for his caution.

Upon the outbreak of that war Roosevelt resigned his position in order to fight; he soon raised a volunteer cavalry regiment that became known as the "Rough Riders." On July 1, 1898, Roosevelt led his men in a charge up San Juan (actually Kettle) Hill in Cuba in one of the most celebrated minor incidents in American military history. Following the war Roosevelt won election as governor of New York State before running for vice president on McKinley's Republican ticket in 1900.

Following McKinley's death Roosevelt was sworn in as president on September 14, 1901. He was not yet quite 43 years old, the youngest man to serve as president. Roosevelt became well-known for his efforts to control trusts and prevent economic monopolies during his presidency. In 1902, for example, the federal government sued the giant Northern Security Company, and in 1904 the Supreme Court ruled in favor of the government, dissolving the company. Roosevelt also intervened in the coal miners' strike in Pennsylvania in 1902, threatening to use federal soldiers to operate the mines if the strike were not ended. Due to this show of potential force, the bargaining committees of both sides came to an agreement and ended the strike. It was a prime example of Roosevelt's toughness.

Similarly, in foreign policy Roosevelt did – in his own words – indeed "carry a big stick." When the Colombian government rejected his offer for land in which to build a canal, Roosevelt supported a revolution against that government, and the new Panamanian officials quickly agreed to the United States' terms. This creation of a inter-ocean canal, uniting the Atlantic and Pacific fleets, was Roose-

velt's proudest accomplishment.

Roosevelt won re-election handily in 1904 after he called on the voters to support his "Square Deal" policies. During his second term Roosevelt worked to pass the Meat Inspection Act and the Food and Drug Act. In 1906 he became the first American to win a Nobel Peace Prize, in recognition of his having mediated negotiations between Russians and Japanese after the War of 1905. In 1907 he sent 16 United States battleships around the world on a good will tour. By the time he left office in 1909 Roosevelt had already handpicked his successor, William Howard Taft, who had been secretary of war. Then Roosevelt went to Africa on a big-game hunt.

In 1912, however, Roosevelt ran against his own former favorite, and when he failed to win the Republican nomination, Roosevelt ran as the candidate of his own Progressive or 'Bull Moose Party". Because he had split the Republican Party, Woodrow Wilson won the election. Roosevelt was highly critical of Wilson, who, he felt, was too slow in bringing the United States into World War I. Roosevelt died of a blood clot shortly after the war ended, on January 16, 1919.

Left: Roosevelt poses with his "Rough Riders" atop just-captured San Juan (Kettle) Hill in July, 1898, during the Spanish-American War.

Left: Roosevelt with his wife, Edith, and their children: (l to r) Quentin, Ted, Archie, Alice, Kermit and Ethel.

47

William Howard Taft

(1857-1930)

Twenty-seventh President of the United States

Term of Office: March 4, 1909-March 4, 1913
First Lady: Helen Herron
Vice President: James S. Sherman

Right: The mountainous twenty-seventh president at a political rally.

Wiliam Howard Taft never truly wanted to be president; he wanted to be chief justice of the United States instead. He did finally attain that position, but first he went through a difficult presidency that was under the shadow of the recently departed Theodore Roosevelt.

Taft was born in Cincinnati, Ohio, on September 15, 1857. His father and grandfather had both been judges. Taft was affectionately called "Big Lub" by his siblings, due to his large size: later, as president and chief justice, Taft would weigh anywhere from 300 to 330 pounds. He was graduated second in his class at Yale and then received his law degree from Cincinnati Law School in 1880. In 1886 he married Helen Herron, who bore him three children.

Helen Taft was very ambitious for her husband and urged him to seek public offices. Taft did serve as solicitor general for the United States, and then as governor of the Phillipines from 1900-1904. His administration was considered a model of careful planning and intelligence. Taft also served as Roosevelt's secretary of war before winning the presidential election in 1908.

Taft created the Tariff Board to undertake the first scientific investigation of the pros and cons of tariffs. In addition to ending the second American occupation of Cuba, he also negotiated treaties of arbitration between Great Britain and France: although the Senate eventually rejected these treaties, they remain testaments to Taft's idealism. Taft also carried on the tradition of "trustbusting," but his efforts seemed inadequate to Theodore Roosevelt, and in 1912 Roosevelt's third-party candidacy ensured Taft's loss in the election – in fact, Taft won only eight electoral votes. But he was not dismayed; rather, he was relieved to be away from the burdens of the presidency.

He became a professor of law at Yale, and in 1921 President Harding appointed Taft chief justice of the United States, making him the only man ever to hold both the nation's highest executive and judicial offices. Taft was delighted with his new position and served faithfully in that capacity until a month before his death on March 8, 1930.

Woodrow Wilson

(1856-1924)

Twenty-eighth President of the United States

Term of Office: March 4, 1913-March 3, 1921
First Ladies: Ellen Louise Axson, Edith Bolling Galt
VicePresident: Thomas R. Marshall

Right: A campaign van in 1916 lists reasons why voters should give Wilson a second term.

Woodrow Wilson was a complex and some- times misunderstood man. Although he did not learn to read until the age of nine, he ulti- mately became the president of Princeton Uni- versity and then the nation's foremost scholar- turned-politician. Although he was a Southerner and had seen the effects of the Civil War, Wilson brought the United States into World War I and then tried to usher in a new world order, based upon the League of Nations.

Wilson was born on December 29, 1856, in Staunton, Virginia, the third of four children of a Presbyterian minister. Wilson's earliest years were clouded by the Civil War, and he later noted that the war had had a profound impact upon him. In 1879 he was graduated from Princeton University, and, after a brief time in law school and an effort at starting his own law practice, Wilson entered grad- uate study at Johns Hopkins University. He re- ceived his Ph.D. in 1886 and then taught at Bryn Mawr and Wesleyan colleges before becoming a professor at Princeton in 1890. He had also mar- ried Ellen Louise Axson. The couple eventually had three daughters.

In 1902 Wilson was appointed president of Princeton University. From this point on, he re- mained in the public eye – and often in the midst of controversy. As the university president Wilson sought to make the campus more democratic by breaking up the exclusive eating-clubs. He failed in this effort, and critics would later claim that the stubbornness he showed in this endeavor was typical of the way he approached politics as well. He did not find compromise easy.

In 1910 Wilson resigned the university presi- dency in order to run for the governorship of New Jersey. He won that contest and thus came even more into public view. In 1912 Wilson was nomi- nated by the Democratic convention on the 46th ballot and then went on to defeat the divided Re- publicans in the national elections.

Wilson supported the reformist Underwood Tarrif Act, which lowered tarrif rates on imports and removed tarrifs from major export items. The Federal Trade Commission was created in 1914. In foreign affairs Wilson was more active and decisive than a scholar might have been expected to be. In 1914 he ordered American troops to occupy the Mexican city of Vera Cruz in an effort to under- mine Mexican President Huerta. Later, Wilson sent General John J. "Black Jack" Pershing to pursue the Mexican rebel-cum-bandit Pancho Villa into Mexican territory.

Left: U.S. Marines in Vera Cruz in 1914. The superficial causes of the dispute with Mexico that led the U.S. to this intervention were trivial, but a deeper cause was that Wilson had long wanted to oust Mexican President Huerta because he had not been popularly elected.

Below: As Navy warships crowd the port's harbor, U.S. Marines stand in parade formation in Vera Cruz. That this crisis did not lead to war was due mainly to mediation by foreign powers.

Above: After much soul-searching, Wilson asks Congress to declare war on Germany in 1917.

Below: U.S. troops in the Argonne, September, 1918, in the climactic American campaign of World War 1.

Above: The "Big Four" at the Versailles Peace Conference: (l to r) Lloyd George of Great Britain, Orlando of Italy, Clemenceau of France and Wilson of the United States.

However, when it came to the outbreak of World War I, Wilson was cautious. He declared United States neutrality at first, although the sinking of the *Lusitania* by a German submarine nearly pushed him to war in 1915. In 1916 Wilson was re-elected under the campaign slogan "He kept us out of war."

But that changed when Germany began to intensify submarine warfare against merchant ships, and finally, in 1917, Wilson reluctantly asked Congress for a declaration of war. The request was approved, and American forces eventually played a key role in the defeat of Germany.

Wilson was determined that this war should be the last one, and he went to Paris in 1918 intent on persuading the victorious nations to create a League of Nations to prevent further warfare. Wilson was rapturously greeted by the Parisian crowds, but the leaders of France, Britain, and

Italy distrusted his idealism. Nevertheless, Wilson returned to the United States with a peace treaty that called for a League of Nations. Now he had to persuade the Senate to approve the treaty.

Wilson began a railroad tour, appealing to the American people to support his program for world peace. Afraid that the treaty would be defeated and under extreme tension, he collapsed and then suffered a paralytic stroke on October 2, 1919, after returning to Washington. Thereafter Wilson was largely confined to his house, and his second wife, Edith Galt (his first wife had died in 1914), had to guide his hand as he signed official documents. But Wilson held all the powers of the presidency until March 3, 1921, the end of his term in office.

Thereafter Wilson lived quietly in Washington. He received the 1920 Nobel Peace Prize for his efforts in behalf of world peace. He died on February 3, 1924.

Warren Gamaliel Harding

(1865-1923)

Twenty-ninth President
of the United States

Term of Office: March 4, 1921-August 2, 1923
First Lady: Florence Kling DeWolfe
Vice President: Calvin Coolidge

Harding was a conservative Republican who believed in a limited presidency, and once in office, he allowed Congress to take the initiative in proposing legislation. He did sign peace treaties, but they did not include the creation of a League of Nations. Harding appointed many of his personal friends to important government jobs, and soon an aura of corruption began to gather about this so-called "Ohio Gang." The Teapot Dome Scandal was merely the most sensational of the numerous fraud and corruption cases involving the president's associates.

In June, 1923, Harding went on a speaking tour across the country. He became depressed following his receipt of a message regarding further Senate investigations of possible corruption in his administration, fell ill in Seattle, and was diagnosed as suffering from pneumonia. On August 2, 1923, Harding died, but no autopsy was performed, and the exact cause of his death is still uncertain. His widow, who burned his correspondence in an effort to preserve his reputation, died the year after her husband, in 1924.

JUGGERNAUT.

Right above: A cartoon shows Attorney General Daughtery and Harding (r) fleeing before yet another scandal.

Right below: Secretary of the Interior Albert B. Fall (l). Convicted of bribery, he was the first cabinet member to go to jail.

Warren Harding is generally regarded as one of the weakest and least-effective of the presidents. A genial and "presidential-looking" man, Harding lacked the motivation to be a true chief executive. When he died in 1923 his administration was almost completely discredited, although there was still some residual popular sentiment for Harding himself.

Harding was born in Corsica, Ohio, on November 2, 1865, the oldest of eight children. He edited his high school newspaper, then taught school and read law before he turned to journalism. In 1891 he married Florence DeWolfe, a banker's daughter. The couple had no children. Mrs. Harding was ambitious for her husband and prompted him to seek office. Harding was a state representative, lieutenant governor, and a United States Senator before being nominated for the presidency in 1920. Harding and Calvin Coolidge ran on a Republican campaign promise to return to "normalcy" in national affairs. Perhaps in reaction to the tumultuous years of World War I, the American public voted for the "normalcy" apparently represented by Harding and Coolidge.

Calvin Coolidge

(1872-1933)

Thirtieth President of the United States

Term of Office: August 3, 1923-March 3, 1929
First Lady: Grace Anna Goodhue
Vice President: Charles G. Dawes

Coolidge was elected mayor of Northampton and served in the Massachusetts senate before being elected governor of Massachusetts in 1918. Although personally shy and taciturn, Coolidge was capable of acting boldly when he perceived a danger to the public interest. He came to national prominence in the Boston Police Strike of 1919 when three-quarters of the city police force went on strike and the city was in considerable danger from looters. Coolidge called up the state guard and crushed the strike, commenting that there was "no right to strike against the public safety." His uncompromising stance was widely applauded and brought Coolidge enough recognition to land him on the Republican party ticket in 1920 as the vice-presidential nominee.

Following President Harding's death in August, 1923, Coolidge was sworn into office by his father, in the middle of the night, in Plymouth Notch, Vermont. Coolidge soon removed the aura of corruption that had gathered in Washington by forcing the resignation of all suspected profiteers left over from the Harding administration. Coolidge also reduced both taxes and the national debt, but he made no effort to dampen the giddy rise of speculation in the stock market. In 1924 Coolidge won the presidency in his own right, using the slogan "Keep Cool with Coolidge."

During his second term Coolidge improved relations with Mexico and helped to foster the Kellogg-Briand Pact, which outlawed war. But whatever pleasure he took in presidency was ruined for him when his son Calvin died of blood poisoning from an infected blister. Coolidge recorded that neither the power nor the glory of the presidency had any appeal for him after his son's death, and in 1927 Coolidge issued a terse statement to the press, declaring that "I do not choose to run for president in 1928." There seems little doubt he could easily have won that election.

Coolidge returned to Northampton and lived the remainder of life quietly. He was affected and saddened by the stock market crash in 1929 and by the Great Depression that followed. He died on January 5, 1933, of a heart attack. His widow survived him by nearly 30 years.

Calvin Coolidge seemed an incongruous president. A tight-lipped, conservative Yankee, he presided over the Roaring Twenties, a time of wild speculation and free-wheeling values. Yet somehow this dour, reticent man struck a responsive chord in the American people, and he was remarkably popular throughout his presidency.

Coolidge was born on Independence Day, 1872, in Plymouth Notch, Vermont. His father had held several political offices. Coolidge attended Amherst College and read law before setting up his own law practice in Northampton, Massachusetts. He then served as the city councilor and city solicitor. In 1906 he married Grace Goodhue, a teacher of deaf children. The couple had two sons.

Right: Calvin Coolidge, with typical enthusiasm, throws out the first ball of the 1927 major league season.

Herbert Clark Hoover

(1874-1964)

Thirty-first President of the United States

Term of Office: March 4, 1929-March 3, 1933
First Lady: Lou Henry
Vice President: Charles Curtis

spent living with relatives. At the age of 17 he entered Stanford University, where he met his future wife, Lou Henry, and decided to become a mining engineer. Hoover worked with a San Francisco firm after his graduation, and in 1898 he and his wife traveled to China, where Hoover had been named chief engineer for the Chinese Mines Bureau. During the Boxer Rebellion of 1900 Hoover directed the distribution of food supplies to the foreigners at Tianjin. This was the first of numerous relief efforts which he would lead.

Hoover then established his own engineering firm and was a self-made millionaire by 1914, when World War I broke out. Early in the war Hoover set up a Commission for Relief in Belgium and later headed the United States Food Administration. To "Hooverize" came to mean saving food which might be used for the national good, and Americans chose to accept "meatless" and "wheatless" days in order to sacrifice for the nation while it was at war.

Hoover served as secretary of commerce under both Harding and Coolidge before being nominated for the presidency in 1928 by the Republican Party. He won the election handily, perhaps because he seemed to represent the prosperity that had persisted through the middle and late 1920s. But the super-heated stock market crashed in October, 1929, just months after Hoover took office. He called business, industrial, and labor leaders for emergency conferences, but he privately believed that the depression would resolve itself and that the federal government should not intervene in the processes of the economy.

As the depression worsened Hoover rapidly lost popularity. Clumps of shacks which were housing to thousands of Americans became known as Hoovervilles. He lost more popularity in 1932 when an army of veterans of World War I marched to Washington to ask for an early distribution of government bonds: the House of Representatives agreed to the disbursement, but the Senate refused, and when rioting began, Hoover ordered in federal soldiers who drove away the Bonus marchers. Many people considered the administration's handling of the affair both precipitate and callous.

In 1932 Hoover was re-nominated by the Republican Party, but he was overwhelmingly defeated by Franklin Roosevelt. It is an irony that Hoover was now believed to be insensitive to the suffering of the American people, for he had been deeply involved in humanitarian causes for over 30 years.

In his retirement Hoover wrote much and spoke often, and, he was again involved in relief action after the end of World War II. By the time of his death on October 20, 1964, he had largely restored himself to the favor of the American public.

H erbert Hoover was remarkably successful as an engineer and as an organizer for the cause of humanitarian relief. His strong moral principles and committment to public service made him stand out both before and after his Presidency. But as president, Hoover had the misfortune of having to face the Great Depression without having any clear recipe for dealing with such a calamity.

Hoover was born on August 10, 1874, in West Branch, Iowa. Both of his parents had died by the time Hoover was nine, and his adolescence was

Right: Jobless men in Washington, D.C., are given relief packages during the Depression.

Franklin Delano Roosevelt

(1882-1945)

Thirty-second President of the United States

Term of Office: March 4, 1933-April 12, 1945
First Lady: Eleanor Roosevelt
Vice Presidents: John N. Garner, Henry A. Wallace, Harry S Truman

Franklin Roosevelt was an unusually powerful and active president whose influence was felt the world over by the end of his time in office. He came from a patrician background and could be domineering, but he also had the common touch. His legacy of social activism and American leadership in world affairs left a deep imprint on American history.

Roosevelt was born in Hyde Park, New York, on January 30, 1882, the son of a wealthy railroad vice president. Roosevelt enjoyed all the privileges of his position as the only child of monied and cultivated parents. He was educated at home until the age of 14 and went on yearly trips to Europe. He was graduated from the Groton School in 1900 and entered Harvard, where, among other things, he became editor of the *Harvard Crimson*. Though he subsequently attended the Columbia University Law School, he was not really interested in the law. In 1905 he married his distant cousin, Eleanor Roosevelt, who was given away by her uncle, Theodore Roosevelt, then the president.

In 1910 Roosevelt won election to the New York state senate, but it was in 1912 that Roosevelt began his real ascent to power by supporting the candidacy of Democrat Woodrow Wilson against that of Theodore Roosevelt. In 1913 Wilson appointed Franklin Roosevelt assistant secretary of the navy. This position was perfect for him, for he loved ships and was interested in the application of naval power, just as fifth-cousin Theodore Roosevelt had been before him.

Roosevelt became something of a national figure during World War I as the result of well publicized visits to European battlefields, and in 1920 he was nominated for the vice presidency by the Democrats, but his ticket was defeated by Harding and Coolidge. In 1921 Roosevelt was stricken by polio after he fell into cold water while sailing, and in a short time he was unable to use his legs at all. But Roosevelt's personal determination carried him through this physical crisis; he exercised every day and eventually gained enough strength to be able to stand with the use of crutches and braces. In 1926 he bought Warm Springs, Georgia's mineral baths, and offered them at a low cost to other polio sufferers.

Polio did not end Roosevelt's political career; in 1928 he won election as governor of New York state, a position he used to increase public control over utilities and to launch innovative initiatives to cope with the Great Depression that had just erupted. As a result of this, Roosevelt won the Democratic nomination and the presidency in 1932. He was 51 years old.

Roosevelt had promised to take vigorous action against the Depression; he began the process by declaring a temporary "bank holiday" and rushing through Congress a whirlwind of legislation that resulted in the creation of so many new programs and agencies that people began calling them an "alphabet soup." Thus, the Agricultural Adjust-

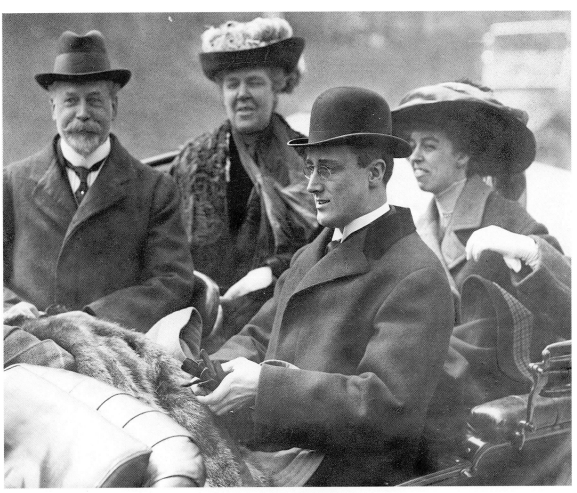

Left: In the foreground, Franklin and Eleanor Roosevelt riding in a carriage in 1913, the year he became assistant secretary of the navy.

Opposite below: F.D.R. and Eleanor Roosevelt in 1918. The children are Anna and James.

Below: Roosevelt, as assistant secretary of the navy, poses with Navy Secretary Josephus Daniels and three navy fliers who set a 1919 transatlantic record.

Right: A 1934 cartoon shows a bemused modern Rip Van Winkle gazing at the "alphabet soup" created by the New Deal.

Below: In 1943 F.D.R. shares a jeep in Sicily with future president Dwight Eisenhower, then Allied commander-in-chief in the area.

ment Act became the AAA, the Tennessee Valley Authority the TVA, and the president himself was soon referred to as FDR. Roosevelt also broke ground in using the new medium of radio to speak directly to the American people in what became known as his "fireside chats." By such means Roosevelt gradually acquired great prestige and popularity. He won a sweeping re-election in 1936, but when he tried to enlarge the Supreme Court, critics claimed that he only wanted to "pack" the court with Democrats.

When World War II began in September, 1939, Roosevelt made it clear that he favored the Allies over the Axis powers, but he read the mood of the country correctly and promised to keep the United States out of the war, even though he took pains to make it possible for the Allies to purchase American weaponry. In 1940 he ran for and won an unprecedented third term in office; he claimed that he needed time to finish what he had begun with the New Deal.

In January, 1941, Roosevelt made his famous "Four Freedoms" announcement: he declared that all people are entitled to freedom of speech and worship, as well as from want and fear. There could by now be no doubt about the depth of his detestation of Hitler and fascism. He may even have been somewhat relieved when, in the wake of the Japanese attack on Pearl Harbor in December, 1941, Hitler and Mussolini imprudently declared war on the United States.

Roosevelt was very much the commander-in-chief during World War II; he had brilliant men as his subordinates, but they all deferred to his character and his judgment. Once American troops had landed in Normandy on D-Day, it was clear that the Allies would win the war, even though there were still dangerous battles ahead. Roosevelt won his fourth term in November, 1944; his campaign had emphasized that America should not switch leaders in the midst of the war. But Roosevelt was worn out from the strain of the war. In February, 1945, Roosevelt attended the Yalta Conference and met for the last time with Churchill and Stalin. He was still perhaps the dominant member of the "Big Three," but his health was fast failing, and he died on April 12, 1945, shortly after collapsing while working at his desk in Warm Springs. Leaders around the world mourned his death and paid tribute to a leader whom they rightly perceived as one of America's greatest presidents.

Below: A haggard F.D.R. poses with Churchill and Stalin in Yalta in 1945.

Harry S Truman

(1884-1972)

Thirty-third President
of the United States

Term of Office: April 12, 1945-January 20, 1953
First Lady: Elizabeth Virginia Wallace
Vice President: Alben W. Barkley

attended business school, and subsequently worked as a clerk and a bookkeeper in various Kansas City banks. From 1906 to 1917 he worked on the family farm, while also becoming a member of the National Guard.

When the United States entered World War I he organized a field artillery regiment and served as its captain, seeing some action in France. After the war Truman and an associate opened a haberdashery in Kansas City; their business prospered

In 1947 Harry S Truman, the son of Missouri farmers, announced that the United States would use its vast military and economic power to help all non-communist peoples prevent the encroachment of communism into their countries. Truman, the first nuclear-age president, was well-prepared, by character and by experience, to back up this commitment – a commitment to which the U.S. would adhere for the next 40 years.

Truman was born in Lamar, Missouri, on May 8, 1884, the oldest of three children. He attended public schools and was an avid reader, perhaps because he felt shy and separated from his classmates because he was near-sighted and wore glasses. He worked in a number of different jobs following his graduation from high school, then for a time, but they had to declare bankruptcy after the business recession of 1921-22. Truman faithfully assumed responsibility for paying off all his business debts; it took him nearly 15 years to do so. Discouraged by business, Truman turned to politics in 1924.

With the support of the Kansas City Democratic political machine Truman became a county judge and then the presiding county judge from 1926 to 1934. (These were not legal positions: he was in effect a commissioner.) Although he remained connected with machine politicians, Truman gained a reputation for honesty and efficiency, and in 1934 he won election to the United States Senate. He was still affiliated with Kansas City boss "Big Tom" Pendergast, so it was not until he won re-election in 1940 that Truman became firmly his own man in a political sense.

During World War II he headed the Committee to Investigate the National Defense; it soon be-

Left: Truman (second row, third from right), poses with his battery in World War I.

*Above: Harry Truman
and friends in Truman's
haberdashery in Kansas
City in the early 1920s.*

came known simply as the "Truman Committee" and so improved American military efficiency that it saved the country $15 billion. During the campaign of 1944 Truman was nominated on the second ballot as Roosevelt's vice-presidential nominee. The pair won the election handily, and upon Roosevelt's death, Truman became president on April 12, 1945.

Truman was not classically well-prepared for the presidency, but he performed remarkably well in the office. In July, 1945, he made the difficult decision to drop the Atomic bomb on Japan and thereby hasten the end of World War II. At Potsdam he met with British Prime Minister Churchill and Soviet Premier Stalin, becoming the newest member of the "Big Three" world leaders. In 1947 he announced the "Truman Doctrine," which declared that the United States would assist countries in their struggles against communist infiltration. Truman also sponsored the Marshall Plan, which offered to assist European countries rebuild their war-shattered economies. He strongly supported the new United Nations and was the first leader to recognize the new state of Israel in 1948.

Truman was less successful in his domestic policy. The Republican majorities in Congress blocked most of his initiatives; and it seemed as if the country were beginning to tire of Democratic leadership and its emphasis on social programs. In 1948 Truman was opposed by Republican Thomas E. Dewey. Nearly all the political pollsters declared that Dewey would win, but Truman went on a 31,000-mile train campaign and surprised everyone by defeating Dewey.

The Korean War broke out in June, 1950, and Truman quickly committed U.S. men and matériel to prevent the conquest of South Korea by communist North Korea. When General Douglas MacArthur, commander of U.S. forces in Korea, criticized Truman's policy of not extending the war to include North Korea's ally, China, Truman dismissed MacArthur from his post.

Truman declined to run for another term in 1952 and chose instead to go into retirement. Although he had been obliged to struggle to find his place in the shadow of Franklin Roosevelt, he is now considered one of the "near-great" presidents. He lived in Independence, Missouri, until his death on December 26, 1972.

Left: Truman, Churchill and Stalin at the 1945 Potsdam Conference.

Below: Truman happily brandishes the famous wrong-guess headline printed by the Chicago Tribune *on the night of Truman's reelection.*

Dwight David Eisenhower

(1890-1969)

Thirty-forth President of the United States

Term of Office: January 20, 1953-January 20, 1961
First Lady: Mamie Geneva Doud
Vice President: Richard M. Nixon

In 1926 Eisenhower was graduated first in a class of 275 officers from the rigorous Command and General Staff School; this accomplishment was the first clear indication of his potential as a leader. Eisenhower was appointed as aide to Douglas MacArthur, the Army chief of staff in 1933. Two years later, Eisenhower drew up contingency plans for a military defense of the Phillipine Islands in case of war.

Just prior to Pearl Harbor, Eisenhower caught the attention of General George Marshall during war games in Louisiana. Eisenhower was promoted to brigadier general in 1941, and in June, 1942, he became the commanding general of American forces in the European Theater. As such, he organized and directed three operations: first, the pivotal American landing in North Africa, and then the Allied invasions of Sicily and Italy. In December, 1943, Eisenhower was given the highest military command the Western democracies could bestow – supreme commander of the Allied forces that were being readied to invade Hitler's "Fortress Europe."

Eisenhower directed the combined American-British efforts in preparation for D-Day in 1944. Landing operations began on June 6, and by the end of the day Allied troops were firmly ashore in Normandy. From that point on, ultimate Allied victory was never seriously in doubt. Eisenhower was not a great tactician, but he had demonstrated that he was a considerable strategist and, above all, a military administrator of near genius.

Following Germany's defeat Eisenhower returned to a hero's welcome in the United States.

Dwight David Eisenhower was highly successful both as the Allied commander in Europe in World War II and as president of the United States. His career demonstrated a remarkable combination of military leadership and political savvy. Eisenhower's personality was his greatest asset; he was usually able to accomplish great results without provoking envy or bitterness among his colleagues.

Eisenhower was born on October 14, 1890, in Denison, Texas, the third of six sons born to deeply religious parents of German and Swiss descent. Eisenhower was popular in high school and worked briefly at a creamery before receiving an appointment to West Point. He was graduated from the Academy in 1915 and married Mamie Geneva Doud in the following year; they had one child, John. During World War I, Eisenhower directed a tank training program for recruits in the United States.

Right: Dwight and Mamie Eisenhower when he was still a junior officer.

Left: General Eisenhower reviews U.S. paratroops hours before the start of the Allied invasion of Europe in June, 1944.

Below: Eisenhower and his vice-presidential running-mate, Richard Nixon, pledge victory at the 1956 Republican National Convention.

REPUBLICAN NATIONAL C

He served as the chief of staff and also as president of Columbia University between 1948 and 1950. In 1952 both the Democratic and Republican parties urged Eisenhower to run for president. He retired from the Army, won the Republican nomination on the first ballot, and defeated Adlai E. Stevenson in the November elections. Eisenhower was the first Republican to be elected president since Herbert Hoover's win in 1928.

Eisenhower championed a "Modern Republicanism" which emphasized fiscal conservatism but which kept in effect most of the social programs that had been developed in the Roosevelt and Truman years. An interstate highway system was one of the more ambitious of the public works projects started during his first term, and by 1956 Eisenhower could even point to a small surplus in the United States Treasury. Indeed, the 1950s were a time of financial growth and personal optimism for many Americans, and Eisenhower seemed to preside over a tranquil country in an appropriate manner – playing golf when he could and demonstrating the relaxed attitude that had gone so far to soothe the tempers and egos of the more volatile American, British and French generals who had served under him in the war.

Yet his easy manner could be deceiving. Eisenhower was as tough a "Cold Warrior" as Truman; with Eisenhower's knowledge, the Central Intelligence Agency overthrew leftist governments in Iran and Guatemala. On the other hand, he disdained to support the domestic red-baiting of

demagogues such as Senator Joseph McCarthy (though, to be sure, critics said he should have done even more to oppose them). By the end of his first term his popularity was still high, guaranteeing re-election, despite his having suffered a heart attack in 1955.

In his second term Eisenhower faced a business recession in 1957-58 and a steady escalation of the Cold War with the USSR. His negotiations with Soviet Premier Khrushchev were broken off when the Soviets downed a U.S. spyplane in their territory in May, 1960, and in January, 1961, Eisenhower terminated diplomatic relations with Fidel Castro's increasingly bellicose Cuban government. When the Soviets took an early lead in the race to put satellites and men into space, Eisenhower called for a crash program of federal assistance to American science education in the public schools. And although it was not publicly known at the time, he was beginning to consult with the CIA about the possibility of overthrowing Castro via a U.S.-sponsored invasion of Cuba by a force of Cuban exiles. This plan was not put into effect before Eisenhower left office in early 1961, but it would cause grave problems for the successor administration.

The Eisenhowers retired to their home in Gettysburg, Pennsylvania, and lived quietly there until Eisenhower died of heart failure on March 28, 1969. For his services to the nation both as a general and as chief executive Eisenhower holds a place in history of considerable distinction.

John Fitzgerald Kennedy

(1917-1963)

Thirty-fifth President
of the United States

Term of Office: January 20, 1961-November 22, 1963
First Lady: Jacqueline Lee Bouvier
Vice President: Lyndon B. Johnson

It might be said that John F. Kennedy was the first "television president." With great skill and charm he was able to present himself as several things: a Boston Irishman, a Harvard man, a World War II hero, and a devoted family man – and at least some of these images had substance. He perhaps had the good fortune of leading the nation when the United States was at the height of its global power and economic predominance, a time when Americans were confident that they could indeed "bear any burden."

Kennedy was born in Brookline, Massachusetts, on May 29, 1917, the second of nine children of multi-millionaire businessman-cum-diplomat Joseph Kennedy and his wife Rose. John attended private schools and Harvard University, and his senior thesis, *Why England Slept,* was published in 1940. During World War II he served in the Navy, and much was subsequently made of an incident in 1943 when his PT boat was rammed and sunk by a Japanese destroyer and Kennedy swam to shore, towing an injured man with him. Kennedy received a Purple Heart for wounds he received in the action.

Following the war Kennedy was elected to the House of Representatives in 1946. His time in the House was not very notable, but in 1952 he ran for, and was elected to, the United States Senate. In 1953 Kennedy married beauteous Jacqueline Bouvier, who became a firm political asset to her husband as well as a fascinating public figure in her own right. In 1956 Kennedy narrowly missed being nominated for the vice presidency and then set his sights on the presidency for 1960.

Kennedy performed admirably in the famous television debates with Republican candidate Richard Nixon in 1960. His cool, mature manner persuaded voters who had previously doubted whether someone so young (43) and a Roman Catholic could serve creditably as president. Even so, Kennedy won the election by the narrowest of margins.

His administration began inauspiciously with the "Bay of Pigs Affair" in which, in April, 1961, CIA-trained Cuban rebels failed disastrously in an attempt to oust Cuban dictator Fidel Castro. (To be sure, the plan had been hatched in the Eisenhower administration, but presumably Kennedy could have stopped it.) In June, 1961, Kennedy met his Soviet counterpart, Nikita Khrushchev, in Vienna. Khrushchev apparently felt that Kennedy was weak-willed and would be an easy mark in the future. He was mistaken; Kennedy was a dedicated "Cold Warrior" who was working to isolate Castro and to increase American military presence in South Vietnam.

In October, 1962, Kennedy led the nation through the Cuban Missile Crisis. On learning that

Russian missiles were being installed in Cuba within range of the United States, Kennedy imposed a blockade of Cuba and then confronted Khrushchev so threateningly that the Soviets agreed to remove their missiles from Cuba. The world had come dangerously close to the nuclear war it had so long dreaded.

In 1963 Kennedy concluded treaty arrangements with the Soviets to limit the testing of nuclear weapons. He was now clearly considered the leader of the "Free World," and his popularity among Americans was high, even though he had yet to accomplish much domestically. But on November 22, 1963, Kennedy was shot and killed by Lee Harvey Oswald in Dallas. Official investigations concluded that Oswald acted alone, but many people still argue that Kennedy must have died at the hands of a conspiracy. His widow's composure and dignity at the funeral impressed the American public once more. Although in the years following his death the Kennedy legend has lost some of its lustre, many people still look back a little wistfully to the undeniable dash, style, and glamour that the Kennedy administration brought to the White House.

Above: Kennedy listens as the first American to make a manned space flight, Alan Shepard, makes his acceptance speech at a 1961 White House awards ceremony. Jacqueline Kennedy is second from the right.

Opposite below: The famed American artist Norman Rockwell painted J.F.K. as an inspiring Peace Corps leader.

Left: In the East Room of the White House an honor guard salutes the casket of the slain John F. Kennedy.

69

Lyndon Baines Johnson

(1908-1973)

Thirty-sixth President of the United States

Term of Office: November 22, 1963-January 20, 1969
First Lady: Claudia Alta (Lady Bird) Taylor
Vice President: Hubert H. Humphrey

Lyndon Baines Johnson has often been denigrated for his policy in Vietnam, for his imprudent fiscal policies, and for his uncouth, dominating personality. This should not obscure the fact of his being a progressive leader who worked toward freeing the United States from hunger, poverty, and racism.

Johnson was born on August 27, 1908, near Stonewall, Texas. His father was alternately a farmer, a schoolteacher, and a state legislator. Johnson was graduated from high school in 1924 and spent nearly three years doing odd jobs and manual labor before attending Southwest Texas State Teachers College. He taught school briefly and then went to Washington, D.C., as a Congressional secretary. Between 1935 and 1937 he served as administrator for a public works program in Texas, and in 1937 he was elected to the House of Representatives.

Johnson served as a lieutenant commander in the U.S. Navy in World War II and then won election to the Senate in 1948. Largely because of his almost uncanny understanding of legislative politics, Johnson held the position of majority leader from 1955 to 1961 and then, as Kennedy's vice president, served as president of the Senate until the time of Kennedy's assassination in November, 1963.

As president, Johnson declared a national War on poverty and saw the Civil Rights bill become law in 1965. His concept of a "Great Society" was popular with voters and brought him re-election in 1964, but growing U.S. involvement in the war in Vietnam was already beginning to affect his presidency.

Following skirmishes between U.S. and North Vietnamese warships in the Gulf of Tonkin, Johnson increased the American military presence in South Vietnam (from approximately 16,300 Americans in 1963 to 500,000 in 1968), and the issue came to dominate the American political scene. There had been unpopular wars before, but none like this, in which an affluent middle class combined with disaffected minorities and a large student population to create a major anti-war movement. Johnson was eventually heckled by protestors who called out, "Hey, hey, LBJ, how many kids did you kill today."

In March, 1968, Johnson announced that he would not seek another term. He retired to his Texas ranch and lived there until he died of a heart attack on January 22, 1973.

*Above: On a visit to
Vietnam in December,
1967, Lyndon Johnson
decorates a U.S. soldier.*

*Opposite below: L.B.J.
signs the Civil Rights Act
of 1964.*

*Left: This picture of
Johnson in retirement on
his Texas ranch was taken
approximately a year
before his death.*

Richard Milhous Nixon

(1913-)

Thirty-seventh President of the United States

Term of Office: January 20, 1969-August 9, 1974
First Lady: Patricia Ryan
Vice Presidents: Spiro T. Agnew, Gerald R. Ford

Nixon practiced law and moved to Washington, D.C., when World War II began. He worked for the Office of Price Administration and served as a naval lieutenant commander in the Pacific. In 1946 Nixon won election to the United States House of Representatives and then moved on to the Senate in 1950, both elections following hard-fought political campaigns.

In 1952 Dwight Eisenhower selected Nixon to be his running mate in the presidential elections. They won, and Nixon served as vice president with distinction for eight years. His string of political successes was ended abruptly by John Kennedy, who defeated him in the 1960 presidential elections after having outshone Nixon in a series of television debates. Following his subsequent loss of the California governor's race in 1962, Nixon announced his retirement from politics.

His sojourn from politics ended in 1968, when he sought the presidency again; this time he captured the office by defeating Democrat Hubert Humphrey by a narrow margin. Nixon was a political and fiscal conservative who nevertheless "thought big" and was able to take calculated risks such as instituting mandatory wage and price controls to fight inflation. It was in his administration, in 1969, that American astronauts landed and walked on the moon, the first men to do so.

It is not easy to categorize Richard Nixon or his political career. He was a complex man who enjoyed moments of political and diplomatic triumph as well as agonizing election losses and the humiliation of resignation from the Oval Office. In retirement he has again proven to be resilient and has, to some extent, rehabilitated his reputation.

Born on January 9, 1913, in Yorba Linda, California, Nixon was the second of five sons. His father worked at a number of jobs, including raising citrus crops and running a gas station-cum-grocery. Nixon was graduated second in his class from Whittier College and went on to Duke University Law School on a scholarship. He was an excellent student and a vigorous debater.

Nixon was also ready to take political risks in his foreign policy. In conjunction with his closest advisor, Henry Kissinger, Nixon began American troop withdrawls from South Vietnam, and, in 1972, he visited the People's Republic of China. His success in opening the door to normalized relations between the United States and Communist China is considered one of his great achievements.

Nixon won re-election by an overwhelming margin in 1972, but during the campaign agents of his re-election committee secretly broke into and burgled Democratic campaign headquarters in the Watergate building in Washington, D.C. The ensuing "Watergate" scandal brought down Nixon's presidency. He denied any part in illegal actions and also denied that there was any attempt to "cover-up" such an involvement, but when tapes were released that implicated officials at all levels of the administration Nixon, rather than face impeachment proceedings, chose to resign from the presidency on August 9, 1974. In retirement Nixon wrote, lectured, appeared often on television, and was occasionally consulted by Republican leaders for his opinions. If he could not hope ever to dissipate the memory of Watergate completely, he nevertheless did a remarkable job of consigning that unhappy episode to the background of the public's consciousness.

Above: Nixon appears on television to give his version of his role in the Watergate affair.

Left center: On China's Great Wall, Richard and Pat Nixon pose for a picture with Chinese leaders during Nixon's historic 1972 visit.

Left: On August 9, 1974, Nixon announced that he had decided to resign from the presidency.

73

Gerald Rudolph Ford

(1913-)

Thirty-eighth President
of the United States

Term of Office: August 9, 1974-January 20, 1977
First Lady: Elizabeth Bloomer Warren
Vice President: Nelson A. Rockefeller

and the University of Michigan before going on to Yale University as a football and boxing coach, as well as a law student. He served in the navy during World War II and then resumed his law career. In 1948 he won election to the House of Representatives and remained there for 25 years, eight of which were in the position of minority leader. When scandals threatened Vice President Spiro Agnew in 1973, President Nixon asked Ford to serve as the new vice president. Upon Nixon's resignation in August, 1974, Ford thus became the chief executive.

Ford worked to fight inflation with a WIN ("Whip Inflation Now") program. He was generally successful, though not very innovative, in foreign affairs, but his major contribution was that he restored the reputation of the presidency after the disgrace of Nixon. Americans liked and trusted Ford, even though he lacked the brilliance of several other recent presidents, and by the time of the American Bicentennial in 1976 the country felt a certain sense of "normalcy" again. However, Ford lost his bid for election in 1976, although by a narrow margin.

Right above: President Ford in his younger days playing football at the University of Michigan.

Right below: Ford is sworn in by the Chief Justice, Warren Burger, on August 9, 1974.

Gerald Ford seemed ideally suited to be a member of the House of Representatives, but a series of unforeseeable circumstances brought him to the vice presidency and finally to the highest office. His legacy is one of repair; he restored dignity and importance to the presidency at a time when its prestige had fallen low.

Ford was born on July 14, 1913, in Omaha, Nebraska. His parents were divorced two years later and his mother re-married; his step-father was a paint salesman. Ford attended public schools

James Earl (Jimmy) Carter

(1924-)

Thirty-ninth President of the United States

Term of Office: January 20, 1977-January 20, 1981
First Lady: Rosalynn Smith
Vice President: Walter F. Mondale

Right: A beaming Carter looks on as erstwhile enemies Anwar Sadat of Egypt (l) and Menachem Begin of Israel shake hands at the Camp David Peace Talks in 1978.

Jimmy Carter showed integrity and tenacity during a difficult presidency. For better or worse, he articulated and pursued the goal of governing by principle rather than by expediency. To some Americans, Carter represented a needed spirit of reform following Vietnam and Watergate, but others came to feel that he sometimes put principle above common sense. His term began with high hopes but ended under the shadow of the hostage crisis in Iiran.

Carter was born on October 1, 1924, in Plains, Georgia. His father was a farmer and businessman. Carter attended local public schools and Georgia Southwestern College before being appointed to the United States Naval Academy. Following his graduation in 1946, Carter married Rosalynn Smith; the couple had four children. Carter worked as an engineer in the new "nuclear Navy" but returned to Plains when his father died and took over the running of the family peanut farm. Gradually his was drawn into local politics and became known for his strong opposition to segregation. In 1962 Carter was elected to the Georgia senate. In 1966 he ran for the governor's seat but lost in the primary. Carter vowed to reverse this setback, and in 1970 he won the gubernatorial election. He soon made a national reputation as one of the progressive governors of the "New South," but few professionals gave him much chance when he announced his intention to run for the presidency in 1976.

Surprisingly, Carter defeated 10 Democratic opponents in the primaries and then edged past incumbent President Ford in the November elections. Carter's first act in office was controversial – he pardoned all draft evaders from the Vietnam era – but otherwise, both he and the nation felt relatively relaxed when his term began in 1977. But by 1978 the national economy was running into trouble, and matters worsened in 1979, with inflation beginning to rise to alarming levels. This was bad enough for the Carter presidency, but a much more serious crisis would soon develop in the arena of foreign affairs.

Carter was idealistic in his foreign policy. He both spoke out strongly against human rights violations everywhere in the world and tried to reduce Cold War tensions. His greatest success came in 1978 when Egypt and Israel signed a peace treaty at Camp David, in part mediated by Carter. But if the Middle East gave him his most memorable triumph, it also ruined him. In November, 1979, Iranian revolutionaries seized the United States Embassy in Teheran and held 53 Americans as hostages. Carter viewed it as of paramount importance to ensure the safe return of the hostages. In the process, American foreign policy, and the American public confidence fell "hostage" to events in Iran. A rescue operation was attempted in April, 1980, but it met with failure and loss of eight American lives.

In 1980 Carter held off a challenge from within the Democratic Party by Edward Kennedy, but Carter lost the election to Ronald Reagan, the former governor of California. Carter returned to Plains, Georgia, but continued to maintain a prominent role as activist and spokesman for liberal causes and human rights.

Ronald Wilson Reagan

(1911-)

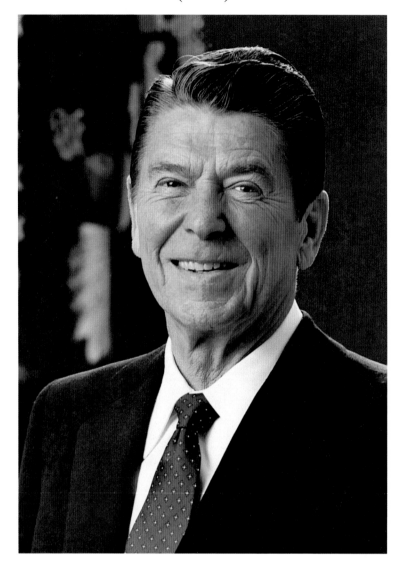

Fortieth President
of the United States

Term of Office: January 20, 1981-January 20, 1989
First Lady: Frances Robbins Davis
Vice President: George H. W. Bush

R onald Wilson Reagan was an actor who became president, a Democrat who became Republican at the age of 51. He stood for "supply-side economics" and fiscal conservatism. He put an end to the fulminating inflation of the Carter years, but his two administrations piled up the largest budget deficits in American history.

Reagan was born on February 6, 1911, in Tampico, Illinois. His mother encouraged his interest in theater, and, after graduation from Eureka College, he became a radio sports announcer in 1932. In 1937 Reagan traveled to Hollywood and had a screen test which led him to a 27-year film career in which he appeared in some 50 movies. In 1947 he became the president of the Screen Actors Guild, a post in which he worked to remove suspected communists from the film industry in the 1950s. Reagan also served as a public-relations representative for General Electric before turning to politics in 1966.

Reagan was originally a Democrat, but he changed his party allegiance in 1962 and soon became the spokesman for the conservative wing of the Republican Party. He first won public office in 1966 when he became governor of California. As governor, Reagan tried to slow state spending and pushed through a major welfare reform bill. In 1976 he opposed incumbent President Ford in the Republican Party, but he narrowly lost the nomination. In 1980, however, Reagan outdistanced six other Republicans for the nomination and then defeated Jimmy Carter in the November election.

Reagan called for a period of national renewal, for lower taxes in order to stimulate the economy, and for a resurgence in American pride and military power; he succeeded in all these things. His foreign policy was the most aggressive since that of Lyndon Johnson. American forces invaded Grenada in 1983, and American planes bombed Libya in 1986 after repeated acts of terrorism by Libyan-sponsored terrorists. Regan also tried to have the nation protected by a space-based anti-missile program called the Strategic Defense Initiative.

Reagan's homespun economic philosophies produced mixed results. Inflation dropped, and the American economy throve in the 1980s, but a huge trade deficit developed, and, worse, the budget deficit shot up to unprecedented levels. Yet his personal popularity remained extremely high – high enough to permit him to beat Democrat Walter Mondale in the 1984 election by the largest number of electoral votes (525) in U.S. history. It even survived the Iran-Contra scandal which broke in late 1986: this was a covert operation in which profits from arms sales to Iran were illegally funneled to anti-communist resistance fighters in Nicaragua. Reagan denied knowledge of the scheme, and though many people did not believe him, most seemed prepared not to blame him.

Reagan retired to California in 1989, with his second wife, Nancy Davis. He continued to be an influential voice in the Republican Party.

Left: Reagan meets with Soviet President Mikhail Gorbachev in 1987 to discuss a treaty that will limit intermediate-range nuclear missiles based in Europe.

Opposite below: Reagan, in his acting days, plays the role of a naval hero in a TV play presented by G.E. Theater.

Below: Ronald and Nancy Reagan at the Republican Convention in 1988.

George Herbert Walker Bush

(1924-)

Forty-first President of the United States

Term of Office: January 20, 1989-January 20, 1993
First Lady: Barbara Pierce
Vice President: J. Danforth Quayle

Right: As CIA director, George Bush confers with Senate Foreign Relations Committee Chairman John Sparkman in 1976.

Geoge Bush used his experience in foreign affairs to good effect, but his perceived weaknesses in domestic policy limited his period in the White House to one term. Thus, though in 1991 most U.S. voters were hailing Bush for his role in the Gulf War against Iraq, by 1992 they were blaming him for not doing more to bring the American economy out of a recession.

Bush was born on June 12, 1924, in Milton, Massachusetts, but would spend most of his youth living in Connecticut and Maine. He was graduated from Phillips Academy in 1942 and he soon became the youngest torpedo bomber pilot in the U.S. Navy in World War II; after being shot down and rescued, Bush was decorated for heroism.

After the war Bush attended Yale University and then moved his young family (he married Barbara Pierce in 1946) to Texas, where he was an oil-field supplies salesman and then the co-founder of Zapata Petroleum Corporation. He turned to government service in 1966, first in the House of Representatives, then as ambassador to the United Nations. He was chairman of the Republican National Committee during the Watergate crisis and then was appointed Chief of the United States Liaison Office in China. He also served briefly as director of the CIA. Bush made an unsuccessful run for the Republican presidential nomination in 1980 and received the consolation prize of the vice-presidency for eight years under Ronald Reagan.

In 1988 Bush won the presidency in his own right, handily beating Democrat Michael Dukakis. His conduct of foreign affairs was masterly. Working with his fellow Texan and Cabinet officer, James Baker, he guided the United States during the period of the 1989 revolutions in Eastern Europe and the breakup of the Soviet Union. In 1990-91 he organized an international coalition that defeated the forces of Iraqi dictator Saddam Hussein. But his considerable popularity rapidly waned in 1992 when people began to blame him for doing too little to combat a recession into which the nation's economy had fallen. Bush argued that the recession was part of a natural business cycle and would soon right itself, but not enough voters agreed, and in 1992 Bush's bid for re-election was defeated by Democrat Bill Clinton. Thus, after more than 25 years of meritorious government service, George Bush retired from public life.

William Jefferson (Bill) Clinton

(1946-)

Forty-second President of the United States

Term of Office: January 20, 1993-
First Lady: Hillary Rodham
Vice President: Albert Gore, Jr.

Right: President Bill Clinton with Vice President Al Gore in 1993.

Bill Clinton was known to the American public at large for a relatively short time before his election, but during that period he convinced voters that he was both a populist "outsider" and a political "insider." It remained to be seen whether such labels would adequately characterize his administration.

Clinton was born William Jefferson Blythe IV on August 19, 1946, in Hope, Arkansas. His father had died in an automobile accident three months earlier, and Bill was later adopted by Roger Clinton, his stepfather. He grew up in Hot Springs, Arkansas, and as a youth was inspired by John F. Kennedy, especially after he met Kennedy at the White House in 1963. Clinton went to Georgetown University on a scholarship. With the Vietnam War in full force, he received a temporary exemption from the draft to attend Oxford University as a Rhodes Scholar. He returned to attend Yale Law School and then married a fellow Yale law graduate, Hillary Rodham, in 1975.

He worked on Democratic presidential campaigns in 1972 and 1976, served as attorney-general of Arkansas (1977-79) and then won the gubernatorial race in Arkansas in 1978, at 32 becoming the youngest governor in the nation. He lost the 1980 election, however, thus becoming the nation's youngest ex-governor, and political observers thought his career was over. But Clinton managed a remarkable comeback and regained the governor's seat in 1982. As governor he worked to improve public education and to attract private industry to Arkansas. Although he had numerous critics, he won re-election in 1984, 1986 and 1990.

During his run for the presidency in 1992 he was plagued by charges of marital infidelity and by his own conflicting statements regarding his draft status during the Vietnam War. But his tenacity and his organizational skills prevailed, and he won the Democratic nomination. He then went on to win a three-way election against Republican George Bush and independent candidate Ross Perot.

When he took office in 1993, Clinton seemed to promise a return to liberal policies and government activism, but he soon encountered difficulties when confronted with making good on a number of his campaign promises, and a rash of unforeseen foreign problems threatened to distract him from fulfilling other parts of his domestic agenda. Yet Clinton's political savvy, his intelligent use of expert advice and his ability to reach the public were undeniably impressive and appeared to augur well for his term in office.

INDEX

Page numbers in italics refer to illustrations